Computer Science, Technology and Applications

nova
science publishers
www.novapublishers.com

Computer Science, Technology and Applications

Speech Recognition Technology and Applications
Vasile-Florian Păiş (Editor)
2022. ISBN: 978-1-68507-929-1 (Hardcover)
2022. ISBN: 979-8-88697-179-8 (eBook)

Internet of Everything: Smart Sensing Technologies
T. Kavitha, PhD, V. Ajantha Devi, PhD,
S. Neelavathy Pari, PhD, Sakkaravarthi Ramanathan, PhD
(Editors)
2022. ISBN: 978-1-68507-865-2 (Hardcover)
2022. ISBN: 978-1-68507-943-7 (eBook)

A Beginner's Guide to Virtual Reality (VR) Modeling in Healthcare Applications with Blender
Ho Lun Ho, Ka Yin Chau, PhD, Yan Wan, Yuk Ming Tang, PhD (Editors)
2022. ISBN: 978-1-68507-811-9 (Softcover)
2022. ISBN: 978-1-68507-945-1 (eBook)

Applying an Advanced Information Search and Retrieval Model in Organisations: Research and Opportunities
Maria del Carmen Cruz Gil
2022. ISBN: 978-1-68507-560-6 (Softcover)
2022. ISBN: 978-1-68507-914-7 (eBook)

Neural Network Control of Vehicles: Modeling and Simulation
Igor Astrov
2022. ISBN: 978-1-68507-757-0 (Hardcover)
2022. ISBN: 978-1-68507-916-1 (eBook)

More information about this series can be found at
https://novapublishers.com/product-category/series/computer-science-technology-and-applications/

Jyoti Prakash Patra
and Yogesh Kumar Rathore
Editors

Applications of Artificial Intelligence in the Healthcare Sector

nova
science publishers
www.novapublishers.com

DOI: https://doi.org/10.52305/FBWX5006

Library of Congress Cataloging-in-Publication Data

ISBN: 979-8-88697-502-4

Published by Nova Science Publishers, Inc. † New York

To everyone who made this book possible, I recognize your efforts from the depth of my heart. My Parents, my Wife Sumitra, my Son Yuvraj, Colleagues of the Computer Science and Engineering Department, the Institution head and the faculty members of Shri Shankaracharya Institute of Professional Management and Technology, Raipurwithout you people this book wouldn't have been possible. I dedicate this book to all of you.

Dr. J. P. Patra

I would like to express our sincere gratitude to everyone who made this book possible. My Father Late S.L. Rathore, my Mother, my Wife Pooja, my Son Shivank, my Daughter Priyanshi, all my family members, Colleagues of the Department of Computer Science and Engineering and management of Shri Shankaracharya Institute of Professional Management and Technology, Raipur for their support and timely advice. I gladly dedicate this book to all of you.

Yogesh Kumar Rathore

Contents

List of Figures

List of Tables

Preface

This book is intended to present a variety of detailed applications of Artificial Intelligence, the Internet of Things, and Robotics in the field of Healthcare. In this book, we have discussed the past and future of Artificial Intelligence in the field of medicine, pharmacy, and Healthcare. this book also focuses on how Artificial Intelligence may play a vital role to save lives in rural areas. In today's era, Artificial Intelligence become an integral part of the pharmaceutical and drug manufacturing industries to detect the drug life cycle and drug composition, with the help of this book we focus on all these aspects.

This book included various experimental results of k-nearest neighbor, support vector machine, decision trees, and other machine learning algorithms applied to detect multiple diseases and process clinical data. We've also included some latest research in the field of Healthcare using deep learning, the Internet of Things, and Robotics. The implementation and applications of IoT and IoRT (Internet of Robotics Things) in Healthcare are also covered in this book. We just had one goal in mind when we created this book: it should be a boon to students who are working in the field of Artificial Intelligence and Healthcare or intend to do so in the future.

Acknowledgments

The completion of this book would not have been possible without the participation and assistance of a large number of persons, many of whose names are not listed. Their contributions are heartily welcomed and appreciated. However, we would like to express our deep appreciation and indebtedness, particularly to the following:

Shri Nishant Tripathi, Chairman (BG), SSIPMT, Raipur, Dr. Alok Kumar Jain, Principal, SSIPMT, Raipur, Dr. Naresh Nagwani, Associate Professor, NIT, Raipur, Dr. Rekh Ram Janghel, Assistant Professor, NIT, Raipur, Dr. Partha Sarathi Khuntia, Principal, KIST, Bhubaneswar, Mr. Tukesh Sahu, data entry operator (DEO), SSIPMT, Raipur for unending support in the formatting of the book.

We are deeply indebted to our colleagues and friends of the Department of Computer Science & Engineering, Shri Shankaracharya Institute of Professional Management and Technology, Raipur for their contribution to bringing out this book. With heartfelt thanks, we remember all those people, though not mentioned here, but have played an important role in the success of this book.

Chapter 1

Artificial Intelligence: Healthcare's Future, Not a Mere Technology

Isha Lingayat*
M. Pharmacy, Clinical Research, Department of Pharmacy Practice
National Institute of Pharmaceutical Education and Research
Sahibzada Ajit Singh Nagar, Punjab, India

Abstract

The chapter aims at providing an aerial perspective on the pressing need for healthcare's innovation: Artificial Intelligence. It puts some light on the limitless scope of AI in healthcare today and what it will bring to the platter tomorrow. Change is the fact of life and advanced technology and tech-savvy personnel have successfully brought that in the form of AI platforms which work wonders in almost every sector. Moreover, AI gained its hype through the revolutionary switch to big data simplifying the discipline of applied science. A brief history, fundamentals, applications, future scope and recent developments where AI turned out to be bliss are broadly covered in the next few pages. Knowledge on yet another domain known as Health economics and outcome research plus real-world studies and how it utilizes AI is penned down as well. In recent scenarios, AI is used in almost every dimension be it education, IT, agriculture, gaming etc. but is bringing a paradigm shift in the healthcare sector in particular. A true boost to the utilization of AI in healthcare is being provided by Pharmacia-informatics in an exceptionally well manner. The chapter aims in highlighting the role of AI during Covid-19 as well. AI's exceptional push in medical imaging, wearable devices, virtual nursing aid, virtual clinical trial, AI-assisted surgery, prescription

* Corresponding Author's Email: isha.lingayat98@gmail.com.

In: Applications of Artificial Intelligence in the Healthcare Sector
Editors: Jyoti Prakash Patra and Yogesh Kumar Rathore
ISBN: 979-8-88697-502-4

auditing, brand management, pricing of drugs and risk control have been avidly elucidated. On-demand AI systems like IBM Watson and other AI systems are superficially illustrated. Mystifying concepts of Artificial intelligence, Machine learning and deep learning are presented in a comparative yet unadorned manner. With numerous opportunities come challenges which are keenly annotated. We conclude with the verity that AI is a mere re-engineering of the human mind and cannot match human intelligence, there are debates and always competition between AI and HI but in actuality, AI is a mere redesigning of the human mind.

Keywords: Artificial Intelligence, machine learning, deep learning, healthcare, medicine

1.1. Introduction

AI has often been accusatively targeted believing that it can gain control over humans but is it really so? The answer is a big no; technology which is backing humans in a number of realms cannot be viewed as a villain. AI is efficient in providing prominent decision-making tools, eventually making human work serene. We often hear that AI improves with experience, here experience indicates data. An easy example is teaching a child to wash hands before every meal. The child will be repetitively asked to do the same until he realizes that doing so is a mark of hygiene (which corresponds to machine learning) and learns to do it by himself/herself (which corresponds to deep learning).

AI is simply educating machines to act like humans. This education signifies algorithmic stuff and covers processes like reasoning, learning, and self-correction.

John McCarthy, Father of AI, claims artificial intelligence is the science and engineering of making intelligent machines, especially intelligent computer programs. Yet another simple definition is given by François Chollet, currently working at Google and creator of Keras deep learning library: "The effort to automate intellectual tasks normally performed by humans" [1].

Sundar Pichai, Google CEO, at a Townhall event in San Francisco in 2018 said: "Artificial intelligence is going to have a bigger impact on the world than some of the most ubiquitous innovations in history". In addition to it, he said that it is going to impact many fields, wherein healthcare being the more prominent one [2].

Frost & Sullivan, a business consulting firm, says artificial intelligence and cognitive computing will save an estimated amount of US$150 billion for the healthcare sector by 2025. It is believed that the implementation of AI will decrease medical costs as there will be more accuracy in diagnosis, better predictions in the treatment plan and better prevention of diseases [3].

1.1.1. History – The Rise of AI

A timeline of events in the history of healthcare is enclosed in the given table 1.1 [4].

Table 1.1. History of healthcare

Year	Event
1950	Alan Turing developed the "Turing test"- a test which tells whether or not a machine can think intelligently like humans or not.
1952	The concept of Machine learning was introduced.
1956	John McCarthy coined "Artificial Intelligence"
1961	Unimate, the first industrial robot ever – a hydraulic manipulator arm installed at a general motors plant at New jersey which could do repetitive tasks.
1964	The first chatbot Eliza was launched.
1966	Shakey, the first electronic person/ mobile robot was launched.
1971	Sir Saul Amarel (AI scientist) at Rutgers University founded a Research resource on computers in biomedicine.
1972	MYCIN: a system which identified severe infection-causing bacteria.
1973	SUMex-AIM is entirely devoted to designing AI applications for the biomedical sciences.
	First AI Winter: mid 1970's-1980
1975	The first NIH (National Institute of Health) sponsored AIM workshop was held
1976	CASNET model for computer-aided medical decision-making is introduced for the first time in a meeting
1980	Development of EMYCIN: advanced version of MYCIN
1986	Release of Dxplain: a diagnostic decision support system which collects clinical information and then derives clinical interpretations.
	Second AI Winter: Late 1980's-early 1990's
2000	Evolution of Deep learning.
2007	IBM Started work to design Deep QA tools
2010	CAD (computer-aided diagnosis) is applied to endoscopy which helps detect colorectal polyps.
2011	"SIRI" The virtual assistance from Apple's integrated for the first time in the i-phones
2014	Amazon's launched its virtual assistant named Alexa.
2015	Pharmabot (pharmaceutical chatbot) was built

Table 1.1. (Continued)

Year	Event
2017	Chatbot Mandy: a kind of communicating agent between patients and doctors wherein the patient answers all the questions in the chatbot which is conveyed to doctors.
2017	Arterys: first FDA-approved cloud-based DL application which gains insights from medical images to make a diagnostic decision and improve efficiency and productivity.
2018-2020	AI trials in Gastroenterology

1.1.2. Conception of Artificial Intelligence and Its Sub-Fields

Domains of Artificial Intelligence are shown in Figure 1.1

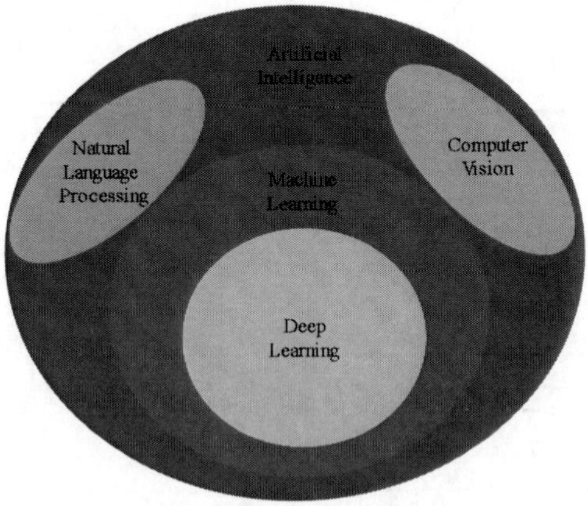

Figure 1.1. Subdomains of AI.

- AI - The term that has created voluminous hype today is a combination of 2 words: "Artificial" which indicates something which is not natural and created by humans and "intelligence" which means the ability to understand or think [5].
- ML – Machine learning simply denotes the ability of the machine to learn by itself automatically. ML models become progressively better by keep on learning through the fed data but still need slight human intervention, unlike DL models [5].
- DL – DL is an evolution of ML. With a DL model, an algorithm can find out whether or not a prediction is accurate through its neural

network—no human help is required. It is an approach for implementing ML [6].

Figure 1.2 illustrates the basic working of deep learning in a pictorial form. The neurons are grouped into three different types of layers:

1. Input layer
2. Hidden layer
3. Output layer

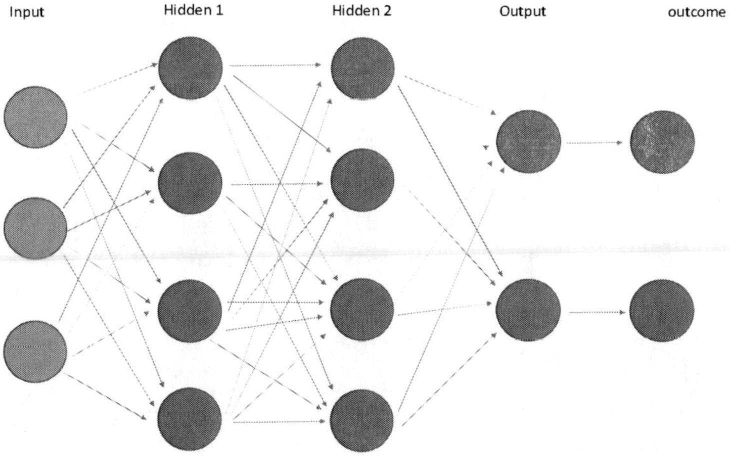

Figure 1.2. Deep Neural Network showing deep learning operation within 2 hidden layers [6].

Here, the task of the input layer is to take data from the input source and send it to the first hidden layer. A Deep Learning model contains so many hidden layers in it which are interconnected with each other to pass information from one node to another node. The hidden layers carry out mathematical operations on the inputs while the output layer generates the output for the user.

- NLP – It is a subset of AI which enables machines to understand and process human/natural languages, to make computers understand human language understanding and thus aid human-machine communication. It allows human language understandable by machines.

Examples –

- Suggestions were given by Predictive typing in Google search
- The spell checker in your email application saves us from silly typing errors.
- Spam mails get excluded on their own by the advanced spam detection feature on mail.
- Siri, Alexa etc. understand natural language through NLP [7].

- Neural Networks – As neurons are to the brain, the neural network is too artificial intelligence [7].
- Computer vision - A revolutionary domain of AI which instructs the computer to understand and analyze the visual world. The concept revolves around the way computers react to digital images and objects and react to it. It resembles a jigsaw puzzle because the computer constructs the images in the same manner as we adjust puzzles to create a meaningful image. The computer is often fed thousands of interrelated images, so as to learn and recognize different features of specific objects. How does it work? Figure 1.3 represents 3 basic steps for the same [7].

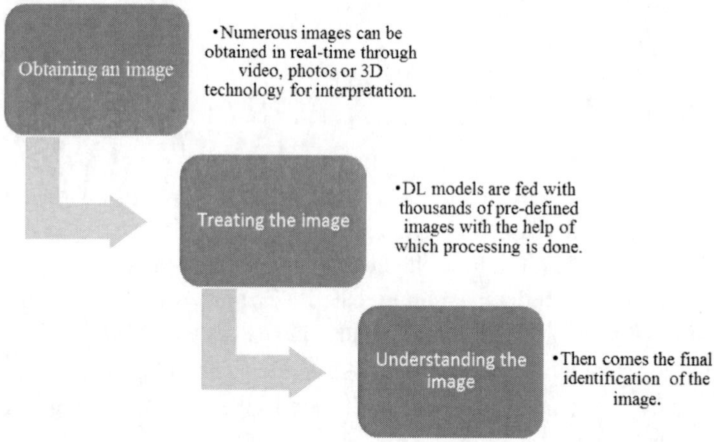

Figure 1.3. Recognising images through the aid of computer vision [7].

- Cognitive computing – It is mimicking human behavior to solve complex problems. No doubt, computers are faster than humans in many ways yet humans conquer the field where these machines lag behind in solving complex problems. Cognitive computing comes into play to solve the issue [8].

1.1.3. AI vs ML vs DL – A Comparative Outlook

ML and DL being the bedfellows of AI need to be understood in a comparative manner for better understanding (See Table 1.2).

1.1.4. Applications of AI in the Healthcare Domain

1. Screening for diabetic retinopathy - 1 in 3 patients with diabetes can develop diabetic retinopathy in their lifetime and timely eye screening can save sight. A system with a robotic camera takes high-resolution images of the retina and diagnostic AI analyses the images for disease and gives an immediate clinical decision: positive or negative for diabetic retinopathy [5].
2. Predicting adverse health events in individual patients – AI techniques and algorithms are used to predict adverse events related to diseases by using preliminary information and thus improving overall patient safety. This aspect of AI especially aids in predicting adverse events from new drug combinations [5].
3. Virtual nursing assistants – Virtual nursing assistance is provided to patients who are recently discharged or under supervision in their home care. They can provide their daily quality of life information to the doctors through this technology and no doubt this is helpful in virtual clinical trials as well [5].
4. Early detection and diagnosis of stroke – Implementing AI algorithms can speed up the process of stroke identification from CT or MR images. Eventually, early detection can improve patient survival [6].
5. Personalized Medicine – A particular disease can be in different forms in different individuals, they shouldn't be treated in the same manner. A person's genomic mutation can be responsible for a disease. If this is the case, precision medicine (the right drug for the right person at the right time) can open up the door to a novel approach to fighting a disease. AI in general aids the designing and development of personalized medicine by analyzing patients' genetic information [9].

Table 1.2. Comparative outlook – AI vs ML vs DL [10, 11]

Properties	AI	ML	DL
Coined in the year	1956	1959	2000
Coined by	John McCarthy	Arthur Samuel	Igor Aizenberg
Conception	An umbrella term with ML and DL as prominent integrants.	Subset/evolution of AI	Subset/evolution of ML. The conception of how deep is machine learning.
Data	-	Data used is in the structured form	Data used is in the form of an artificial neural network.
Definition	The ability of a machine to mimic human behaviour through a set of rules (algorithm). Basically ability of a machine to think.	The ability of a machine to learn on its own, by its own mistakes and past experience by using statistical methods.	A kind of Machine learning that teaches machines to do what comes naturally to humans by using artificial neural networks (inspired by the structure and function of neurons present in the human brain). A large amount of data is fed until it learns by itself.
Sub categories	3 broad types of AI are – Artificial Narrow Intelligence (ANI), Artificial General Intelligence (AGI) and Artificial Super Intelligence (ASI)	3 broad types of ML are – Supervised Learning, Unsupervised Learning and Reinforcement Learning	3 broad categories of deep neural network models are – Pre-trained models, Convolutional Neural Networks (CNN) model, Recursive Neural Networks, and Recurrent Neural Networks (RNN) model
Execution time	-	The training time needed for a machine using the ML technique is less than DL.	The training time needed for a machine using DL is more than ML.
Data dependency	-	For a small amount of data, ML proves to be the best technique to train your machine.	For a large amount of data, DL proves to be the best technique to train your machine.
Efficiency	The efficiency of AI = Efficiency of ML + DL	Less efficient than DL as it can't work for a larger amount of data.	More efficient than ML as it can easily work for larger sets of data.
Data analytics	-	ML consists of thousands of data points.	Big data: millions of data points.

"AI's going to look back on us the same way we look on fossils."

6. Patient record management and information retrieval – information retrieval systems like electronic medical records, electronic patient records, medical diagnosis systems, medical image systems, etc. are rich sources of medical information about the patient [12].
7. Patient Monitoring through wearable devices – Medical fitness trackers, Fitbit, smart watches, ECG monitors and BP monitors are of utmost importance during virtual clinical trials as it collects daily health data of the patients [13].
8. Drug Discovery and development - Drug discovery has always been a kind of trial and error game, 1000's molecules are processed and ultimately just 1 single drug candidate achieves success in the market, which takes around 10 + years. AI is leveraged to accelerate this process wherein the algorithms eliminate the ineffective molecules before the company is going to burns a lot of money. Recently world's first wholly AI-designed drug for Idiopathic Pulmonary Fibrosis (IPF) entered the clinical trial. A company named NuMedii has developed a software named AIDD (Artificial intelligence for drug discovery) that aids drug discovery at a faster pace [13].
9. Infectious disease Surveillance – Timely identification of infectious diseases is necessary for maintaining public health. Majorly the data is collected from social media, news reports, internet-based searches, and specific surveillance systems [14].
10. Prescription auditing – It is worth noting down that, 7000-9000 people die each year due to medication errors in the US alone. An AI system that can identify prescription mistakes and helps in minimizing the same and prevent the same can save no. of lives.
11. Brand management, pricing and risk control – AI algorithms help in determining the optimal price for the treatment and other services according to competition and other market trends [15].
12. Neuro-prosthetics – These are medical devices (chip or electrodes placed on the scalp) that restores neural dysfunctions affected by some pathological conditions. AI is incorporated in these prosthetics which interprets electric nerve signals from the patient's muscles [16].
13. EHR (Electronic health records) and EMR (Electronic medical records) – EHRs and EMRs are electronic versions of a patient's medical history. Patient information saved in EHR and EMR can be used to predict the possibility of diseases with the help of AI algorithms [17].

14. Robot/AI-assisted surgery – It is helpful in monitoring the movement of surgeons during a complex surgical procedure and can provide a kind of prior alert to the surgeons of any mishappening that can take place. Some robots or machines are implemented for the same [18].
15. Diagnosis aid – AI helps in detecting, predicting, and diagnosing diseases more accurately and at a faster rate than humans [19].
16. Virtual clinical trial – Online recruitment of patients for ongoing trials, ongoing screening of patients according to eligibility criteria, e- consent of screened subjects, online randomization of subjects, and remote patient monitoring, reduces a lot of administrative burdens that fall on the physicians while running a clinical trial [19].
17. Medical imaging – It involves MRI scans, and X-rays used to diagnose cancers and tumors which are further reviewed by radiologists for signs and diseases [20].
18. Digital consultation - Health chatbots respond to health-related questions and support patients by providing data on a variety of medications and suggested doses [21].
19. Detecting mental conditions – AI has the ability to detect behavioral signs of anxiety with over 90% accuracy. Activities like nail-biting, knuckle cracking, and hand tapping is noted by motion sensors which manifest mental issues clearly. Speech and language-based signs of mental distress are one of the aspects of AI. Psychiatrists explain that a monotone conversation with a patient can suggest depression, speedy speech can suggest mania, and disjointed words while speaking can indicate schizophrenia. Written language is also one of the promising aspects of AI. ML algorithms instructed to assess word choice and order are far better and quicker than clinicians to distinguish between real and fake suicide notes i.e., they are good at detecting signs of distress. By regularly monitoring patients' writing, AI systems can assess their risk of self-harm [21].
20. Recognition of facial symptoms – unique facial features and expressions are characteristics of some rare diseases popularly known as the phenotyping approach. Face2gene app is becoming a modish tool for recognizing rare diseases [21].
21. Drug creation – The drug discovery and development process takes 10+ years and on top of that billions of US dollars. To make this timely process a bit cheaper and quicker, AI can be availed in some parts of this full-length process. AI can be employed to discover repurposed effects of existing drugs. At the time of the 2014 Ebola

virus outbreak, AI was used to scan possible medicines that might be redesigned to be adopted for the disease [22].

22. Heart lander: a mobile robot – It certainly sounds like a fantasy but a prototype of a miniature robot which has proven its efficacy on a pig's heart can work wonders in near future. A miniature caterpillar sort of robot is placed on the heart, which travels to the desired location and administers the therapy [23].

1.1.5. AI Systems in the Healthcare Sphere

Common AI systems along with their operations are given in tabular format in Table 1.3.

Table 1.3. AI systems in healthcare [24]

S. No.	Systems/Tools	Applicability
1	IBM Watson	It facilitates medical research, clinical research and healthcare solutions for clients.
2	Ada	It's a free mobile app a kind of health companion. It immediately assesses your health condition based on your input regarding your symptoms.
3	Your.MD	Your.MD or healthily provides patients with personalised health information via a chatbot.
4	Third opinion	A company focused on digitizing healthcare and providing better AI services for doctors.
5	Deep Mind Health	UK-based company deep mind collaborated with Google health to form deep mind health which is involved in developing AI research and mobile tools to tackle the healthcare sector's issues.
6	Face2Gene	This AI app analyses 88 points on the face of a person and gives an order of likelihood of various genetic syndromes in a couple of seconds.
7	Botkin AI	It's a software which speeds up the process of analysing radiograms and diagnosing the risks of tumours.
8	Cardiio	An app that monitors heart rate at rest and after exercise using imaging photoplethysmography.
9	HealthifyMe	India's largest digital wellness platform which harnesses AI to offer fitness services.
10	Gymfitty	India's first AI-based personal trainer with pre-recorded workout sessions and tracks your progress. Moreover, it works offline as well.

1.1.6. AI in Health Economics and Outcomes Research

AI offers paramount opportunities in 5 major research activities of HEOR (see Table 1.4):

1. burden of illness
2. Patterns of drug utilization
3. patient-reported outcomes (PRO)
4. comparative-effectiveness research (CER)
5. economic evaluations

Table 1.4. Budding applicability of AI application in the field of HEOR [25]

	Burden of illness	Drug utilization and patterns of use	Patient-reported outcomes	Comparative effectiveness research	Economic evaluations
NLP		+++	+++	+++	
Text data analysis	++		+++		
ML	++	+++		++	+++
DL	+++			+++	

+ sign represents the extent of applicability of a particular AI aspect into HEOR.

1.1.7. AI in Real-World Evidence and Real-World Studies

Evidence is a claim to particular knowledge. In the medical world, this evidence is derived from real-world data regarding the use, benefits and risks of a health technology or it can be regarding a patient's health status and routine delivery of care. This data is derived from a variety of sources but this source can never be a randomized clinical trial. Rather these sources are medical claim databases, electronic health records, electronic medical records, patient registries etc. The data generated through these sources are voluminous and AI makes the task of generating insights from this voluminous data way too easy for patient benefit. The application of AI to real-world studies has potential in drug development, disease prediction, and patient monitoring. One recently applied area is the MIMIC III (Medical Information Mart for Intensive Care) database which contains information on hospital admitted patients. AI implementation here helped to understand patient discharge notes with the help of NLP and then extracted using ML. This helped in predicting the possibility of patient readmission into the hospital [26].

1.1.8. AI: Savior in COVID-19 Pandemic

Right after the disastrous entry of COVID-19, WHO (World Health Organization) declared that AI can work wonders in managing the same.

1. In the prediction and tracking of COVID-19 – AI helped in forecasting the spread of the disease by leveraging information from various online platforms. Blue Dot software helped in identifying the locations with the majority of COVID-19 cases.
2. Contact tracing - Contact tracing can be defined as a process in which people who might have come into contact with an infected person can be traced. Mobile health application AarogyaSetu launched by the Government of India on 2nd April 2020 came into play. Being a contact tracing platform it assisted over 19 crore users worldwide.
3. Early detection and diagnosis of COVID-19 cases – AI tools like medical imaging, X-ray, CT scan, nucleic acid, serologic and vial throat swab testing methods have aided in its early detection and diagnosis. Covid-19 detection neural network (COVNet) - a DL model, was developed for differentiating Covid-19 and community-acquired pneumonia based on 2D and 3D CT scan images [27].
4. Monitoring Covid-19 cases – AI monitors patients in clinical settings and predicts chances of recovery or mortality in covid-19.
5. AI reduced the burden on healthcare personnel and patients – With AI, unnecessary hospital visits were prevented as distant monitoring and the approach of telemedicine were taken into account. AI-based chatbots were used for consultation and reduced the transportation of patients.
6. Protein structure prediction – AI predicts the structure of proteins significant for viral entry and replication. These insights further helped in drug development in a shorter period of time. Alpha Fold algorithm acted as a boon for the same.
7. In the development of drugs – We are familiar with a large amount of time required to bring a drug into the market. AI helped in accelerating the process of lead discovery, virtual screening etc.

involved in drug discovery. AI helped in detecting the repurposing of approved drugs for COVID-19 [28].

1.2. Literature Survey

1.2.1. Recent Developments Where AI Acted as a Bliss

1. An ultrasound image-based AI platform has been developed by researchers at Harvard University to assess whether ultrasound images of a thyroid nodule are cancerous or not. This further assists in the early detection of the tumor stage and nodal stage [29].
2. Scientists at the Mayo Clinic Cancer Centre in Florida have implemented a ML platform which predicts which out of 2 therapies (chemotherapy or immunotherapy) will benefit patients with Gastric Cancer [30].
3. An artificial intelligence platform has been developed by the Massachusetts Institute of Technology that is able to predict almost half of breast cancer incidences up to five years before they happen [31].
4. Researchers from UT Southwestern Medical Centre and the University of Washington utilized an AI platform to produce 3D models of eukaryotic protein interactions [32].
5. Researchers from New York University ad NYU Abu Dhabi claimed that they have come up with an AI platform to identify BC in ultrasound images with an accuracy almost similar to that of radiology [33].
6. A freely accessible AI platform developed by researchers from the University of Bonn helps diagnose leukaemia or lymphoma even in resource-poor settings [34].
7. Researchers at Children's National Hospital have devised a facial recognition tool using the concept of ML which aids in diagnosing rare genetic syndromes like Down syndrome, Noonan syndrome etc. faster. Thus, earlier diagnosis. Differences in facial features of these patients are sometimes clearly visible but many times are subtle to point out [35].
8. Researchers from Johns Hopkins Kimmel Cancer Centre developed a novel AI blood testing technique called DELFI (DNA evaluation of

fragments for early interception) with a claim of detecting more than 90% of lung cancers in almost 800 individuals' samples with and without cancer [36].

9. An early diagnosis of Schizophrenia is promised by a ML algorithmic system developed by researchers at Baylor College of Medicine [37].
10. Researchers at Institute for Research in Biomedicine in Barcelona have developed a ML tool which can assess possible mutations in a particular gene and evaluate the probability of cancer development through it [38].
11. An AI tool called chatbot is used as a healthcare system to help patients schedule appointments and answer their queries related to healthcare insurance. During the pandemic to address Covid related enquiries, scheduling vaccination slots etc. these chatbots have proved as an asset [39].
12. Researchers at the Eindhoven University of Technology successfully developed a system collaborating ML with immunotherapy to find hidden tumor cells in the human body [40].
13. Researchers from IBM and Pfizer have trained the AI model in such a way that it can screen for Alzheimer's disease by simply analyzing writing patterns or linguistic patterns in the use of words [41].
14. Google has launched an AI-based application that helps to identify patients' skin, nail and hair conditions by analyzing its images. It claims to detect 288 skin conditions. However, it has not yet replaced the usual human diagnosis practice [42].
15. Researchers at the European Molecular Biology laboratory have combined AI algorithms with two cutting-edge microscopy techniques which resulted in shortened image processing time from days to mere seconds [43].
16. Researchers have implemented the DL concept to accurately predict samples from Alzheimer's disease suffering patients [44].

1.2.2. Challenges Faced

With opportunities, AI brings few challenges to the healthcare platter. On a positive note, every challenge is an opportunity. The very first hurdle is the availability of large datasets. Large datasets are required to give relevant output through AI and ML-based models. With a huge amount of data comes the responsibility of data privacy and confidentiality. There will always be malicious hackers seeking chances to exploit the patient or hospital information.

Yet another concern that AI will replace jobs is worrying a group of people. This threat is generating less liking for AI-based tools. There are still a lot of positive aspects which people should be made aware of The next concern is in case of any discrepancy occurrence, who should be held responsible – the personnel using the system or the AI system itself? In some countries no AI system is held totally responsible to make decisions, there are always some human inputs to be made parallelly. The complications increase even more when it is realized that there are no specific industry guidelines on the ethical use of AI in healthcare [45].

1.2.3. Future of AI

The majority of the companies you connect to on-call nowadays have IVRS (Interactive voice response system) installed. Be it online shopping websites, banks, doctor consultations, IT companies etc. all have IVR systems. Sometimes, even machines call you! Isn't it great, how the manual workload has been lowered? Driverless cars are one of the next fantasies to get attained in the coming years. We have noted how AI technology RT-PCR analyzed swab specimens and generate results within a few days and sometimes within a few minutes depending upon the test. This specifies how phenomenally AI can come up with its application when humans are in need.

AI's potential to gather a large amount of data is certainly going to act as a boon to the health sector in quickly diagnosing the medical condition in a larger set of populations. More accurate diagnostic results will be obtained. The way diseases are diagnosed, treated, prevented and prescribed for medicines will be more accurate with a broader perspective and fewer complexities, discrepancies and expenses. Rural areas where access to healthcare lags behind can be improved with the help of applied science [46].

1.2.4. Human Intelligence vs Artificial Intelligence – Is the Debate Worth It?

There are debates where competition between AI and Human intelligence is discerned. It is not fair to recognize one superior over another. Both have their own significance. If AI is good at processing data, humans dominate abstract thinking. People are worried that machines will take their jobs. Can't we think about it positively? There have been numerous researches which show beyond doubt that AI has a promising future in the healthcare domain. However, this does not assert that AI will completely replace doctors and nurses but rather affirm how AI can supplement and support healthcare outcomes. Despite the remarkable functionality of AI in healthcare, it is still finite in terms of quality and authenticity of available health data and by lack of possessing human-like characteristics, such as physical touch, compassion and care [46].

Conclusion

Prior few pages have elicited how AI is healthcare's future. With advancements in AI, the world feels like a wonderland. Already no. of areas and applications has been utilized through AI which projects a sure possibility of this ongoing trend to stay continue. AI has the ability to learn by itself through experience and further on without any human intervention (ML and DL) which will constantly keep evolving and these applications will help in the betterment of the patient as a whole. Elon musk says "adopting AI is like summoning the demon". He further adds "AI can provoke World War III". Russian President Vladimir Putin said, "First global leader of AI will turn out to be the ruler of the world". These statements reveal the extent of national competition for AI. With competition comes to progress and with progress comes the betterment of humankind.

References

[1] Rajaraman V. John McCarthy — Father of artificial intelligence. *Resonance* [Internet]. 2014 [cited 18 October 2019];19(3):198-207. Available from: https://www.ias.ac.in/article/fulltext/reso/019/03/0198-0207.

[2] Dick S. Artificial Intelligence. *Harvard Data Science Review* [Internet]. 2019 Jul 1;1 (1). Available from: https://hdsr.mitpress.mit.edu/pub/0aytgrau.

[3] Mesko B. The role of artificial intelligence in precision medicine. *Expert Review of Precision Medicine and Drug Development*. 2017 Sep 3;2(5):239-41.

[4] Kaul V, Enslin S, Gross S A. *History of artificial intelligence in medicine*. 2020 Oct;92(4):807-812. doi: 10.1016/j.gie.2020.06.040. Epub 2020 Jun 18.

[5] Bohr A, Memarzadeh K. The rise of artificial intelligence in healthcare applications. *Artificial Intelligence in Healthcare*. 2020:25–60. doi: 10.1016/B978-0-12-818438-7.00002-2. Epub 2020 Jun 26.

[6] Jiang F, Jiang Y, Zhi H, Dong Y, Li H, Ma S, Wang Y, Dong Q, Shen H,·Wang Y. Artificial intelligence in healthcare: past, present and future. *Stroke and Vascular Neurology*. 2017;2(4):230-43.

[7] Hirschberg J, Manning C. Advances in natural language processing. *Science* [Internet]. 2015 [cited 3 December 2019];349(6245):261-66. Available from: https://pubmed. ncbi.nlm.nih.gov/26185244-advances-in-natural-language-processing/

[8] Mishra M. Computer Vision in Artificial Intelligence [Internet]. *Oracle*. 2019 [cited 3 March 2020]. Available from: https://blogs.oracle.com/datascience/computer-vision-in-artificial-intelligence.

[9] Ragunath g. Understanding The Difference Between AI, ML, And DL: Using An Incredibly Simple Example — Advancing Analytics [Internet]. *Advancing Analytics*. 2021 [cited 30 April 2022]. Available from: https://www. advancinganalytics.co.uk/blog/2021/12/15/understanding-the-difference-between-ai-ml-and-dl-using-an-incredibly-simple-example#:~:text=In%20summary%2C% 20AI%20is%20a,a%20subset%20of%20ML%2.

[10] Bini S A. Artificial Intelligence, Machine Learning, Deep Learning, and Cognitive Computing: What Do These Terms Mean and How Will They Impact Health Care? *J. Arthroplasty*. 2018 Aug;33(8):2358-2361. doi: 10.1016/j.arth.2018.02.067. Epub 2018 Feb 27.

[11] Erickson B J. Basic Artificial Intelligence Techniques: Machine Learning and Deep Learning. *Radiol. Clin. North Am.* 2021 Nov;59(6):933-940. doi: 10.1016/j.rcl. 202106.004.

[12] Bajwa J, Munir U, Nori A, Williams B. Artificial intelligence in healthcare: transforming the practice of medicine. *Future Healthc J.* 2021 Jul;8(2):e188-e194. doi: 10.7861/fhj.2021-0095.

[13] Secinaro S, Calandra D, Secinaro A, Muthurangu V, Biancone P. The role of artificial intelligence in healthcare: a structured literature review. *BMC Med. Inform. Decis. Mak.* 2021 Apr 10;21(1):125. doi: 10.1186/s12911-021-01488-9.

[14] Reddy S, Fox J, Purohit M P. Artificial intelligence-enabled healthcare delivery. *J. R. Soc. Med.* 2019 Jan;112(1):22-28. doi: 10.1177/0141076818815510. Epub 2018 Dec 3.

[15] Vijai C, Wisetsri W. Rise of Artificial Intelligence in Healthcare Startups in India. *Advances In Management*. 2021 Mar 1;14(1):48-52.

[16] Schwalbe N, Wahl B. Artificial intelligence and the future of global health. *Lancet*. 2020 May 16;395(10236):1579-1586. doi: 10.1016/S0140-6736(20)30226-9.

[17] Winter J S, Davidson E. Governance of artificial intelligence and personal health information. *Digital policy, regulation and governance*. 2019 May 13.

[18] Sharma A. Artificial Intelligence in Health Care. *International Journal of Humanities, Arts, Medicine and Science*. 2021;5(1).

[19] Nayak S, Das R K. Application of artificial intelligence (AI) in prosthetic and orthotic rehabilitation. In *Service Robotics* 2020 Oct 7. IntechOpen.

[20] Alugubelli R. Exploratory Study of Artificial Intelligence in Healthcare. *International Journal of Innovations in Engineering Research and Technology*. 2016;3(1):1-0.

[21] Ranschaert E R, Morozov S, Algra P R, editors. *Artificial intelligence in medical imaging: opportunities, applications and risks*. Springer; 2019 Jan 29.

[22] Yu K H, Beam A L, Kohane I S. Artificial intelligence in healthcare. *Nature biomedical engineering*. 2018 Oct;2(10):719-31.

[23] Khanna D. Use of artificial intelligence in healthcare and medicine. *International Journal of Innovations in Engineering Research and Technology*. 2018 Dec.

[24] Chapman M P, Lopez Gonzalez J L, Goyette B E, Fujimoto K L, Ma Z, Wagner W R, Zenati M A, Riviere C N. Application of the HeartLander crawling robot for injection of a thermally sensitive anti-remodeling agent for myocardial infarction therapy. *Annu. Int. Conf. IEEE Eng. Med. Bio. Soc*. 2010; 2010:5428-31. doi: 10.1109/IEMBS.2010.5626518. PMID: 21096276.

[25] Iliashenko O, Bikkulova Z, Dubgorn A. Opportunities and challenges of artificial intelligence in healthcare. In *E3S Web of Conferences* 2019 (Vol. 110, p. 02028). EDP Sciences.

[26] Rueda J, Cristancho R. *Is Artificial Intelligence the Next Big Thing in Health Economics and Outcomes Research?* [Internet]. ISPOR | International Society For Pharmacoeconomics and Outcomes Research. 2022 [cited 2 May 2022]. Available from: https://www.ispor.org/publications/journals/value-outcomes-spotlight/abstract/march-april-2019/is-artificial-intelligence-the-next-big-thing-in-health-economics-and-outcomes-research.

[27] Khan S. *Using AI/ML to Generate Real World Evidence* [Internet]. Iqvia.com. 2022 [cited 2 May 2022]. Available from: https://www.iqvia.com/locations/canada/blogs/2020/08/using-ai-ml-to-generate-real-world-evidence.

[28] Khan M, Mehran M T, Haq Z U, Ullah Z, Naqvi S R, Ihsan M, Abbass H. Applications of artificial intelligence in COVID-19 pandemic: A comprehensive review. *Expert systems with applications*. 2021 Dec 15;185:115695.

[29] Vaishya R, Javaid M, Khan I H, Haleem A. Artificial Intelligence (AI) applications for COVID-19 pandemic. *Diabetes & Metabolic Syndrome: Clinical Research & Reviews*. 2020 Jul 1;14(4):337-9.

[30] Li H, Weng J, Shi Y, Gu W, Mao Y, Wang Y, Liu W, Zhang J. An improved deep learning approach for detection of thyroid papillary cancer in ultrasound images. *Scientific reports*. 2018 Apr 26;8(1):1-2.

[31] Jang H J, Lee A, Kang J, Song I H, Lee S H. Prediction of genetic alterations from gastric cancer histopathology images using a fully automated deep learning approach. *World Journal of Gastroenterology*. 2021 Nov 28;27(44):7687.

[32] Vyborny C J, Giger M L. Computer vision and artificial intelligence in mammography. *AJR. American Journal of Roentgenology*. 1994 Mar;162(3):699-708.

[33] Lim H, Cankara F, Tsai C J, Keskin O, Nussinov R, Gursoy A. Artificial intelligence approaches to human-microbiome protein–protein interactions. *Current Opinion in Structural Biology*. 2022 Apr 1;73:102328.

[34] Rodríguez-Ruiz A, Krupinski E, Mordang J J, Schilling K, Heywang-Köbrunner S H, Sechopoulos I, Mann R M. Detection of breast cancer with mammography: effect of an artificial intelligence support system. *Radiology*. 2019 Feb;290(2):305-14.

[35] Salah H T, Muhsen I N, Salama M E, Owaidah T, Hashmi S K. Machine learning applications in the diagnosis of leukemia: Current trends and future directions. *International Journal of Laboratory Hematology*. 2019 Dec;41(6):717-25.

[36] Li L, Mu X, Li S, Peng H. A review of face recognition technology. *IEEE access*. 2020 Jul 21;8:139110-20.

[37] Espinoza J L, Dong L T. Artificial intelligence tools for refining lung cancer screening. *Journal of Clinical Medicine*. 2020 Dec;9(12):3860.

[38] Cortes-Briones J A, Tapia-Rivas N I, D'Souza D C, Estevez P A. Going deep into schizophrenia with artificial intelligence. *Schizophrenia Research*. 2021 Jun 5.

[39] Bi W L, Hosny A, Schabath M B, Giger M L, Birkbak N J, Mehrtash A, Allison T, Arnaout O, Abbosh C, Dunn I F, Mak R H. Artificial intelligence in cancer imaging: clinical challenges and applications. *CA: a cancer journal for clinicians*. 2019 Mar;69(2):127-57.

[40] Waheed A, Shafi J. Successful role of smart technology to combat COVID-19. In2020 Fourth International Conference on I-SMAC (IoT in Social, Mobile, Analytics and Cloud) (I-SMAC) 2020 Oct 7 (pp. 772-777). *IEEE* [Internet]. 2021 [cited 2 May 2022]. Available from: https://www.genengnews.com/news/using-machine-learning-methods-to-predict-response-to-immunotherapy/

[41] Hsu J. AI Assesses Alzheimer Risk by Analyzing Word Usage [Internet]. *Scientific American*. 2020 [cited 2 May 2022]. Available from: https://www. Scientific american.com/article/ai-assesses-alzheimers-risk-by-analyzing-word-usage/.

[42] Kleinman Z. Google AI tool can help patients identify skin conditions [Internet]. *BBC News*. 2021 [cited 2 May 2022]. Available from: https://www.bbc.com/news/technology-57157566.

[43] Wells A, Patel S, Lee J B, Motaparthi K. Artificial intelligence in dermatopathology: Diagnosis, education, and research. *Journal of Cutaneous Pathology*. 2021 Aug;48(8):1061-8.

[44] Silva-Spínola A, Baldeiras I, Arrais J P, Santana I. The road to personalized medicine in Alzheimer's disease: The use of artificial intelligence. Biomedicines. 2022 Jan 29;10(2):315.Sunarti S, Rahman FF, Naufal M, Risky M, Febriyanto K, Masnina R. Artificial intelligence in healthcare: opportunities and risk for future. *Gaceta Sanitaria*. 2021 Jan 1;35:S67-70.

[45] Buch V H, Ahmed I, Maruthappu M. Artificial intelligence in medicine: current trends and future possibilities. *British Journal of General Practice*. 2018 Mar 1;68(668):143-4.

[46] Dutta A. *AI, the Biggest Existential Threat to Humankind says Elon Musk* [Internet]. Analyticsinsight.net. 2021 [cited 2 May 2022]. Available from: https://www. analyticsinsight.net/ai-the-biggest-existential-threat-to-humankind-says-elon-musk/.

Chapter 2

Applications of Artificial Intelligence in Rural Areas

Somesh Dewangan[1,*], Siddharth Choubey[1,†], Jyotiprakash Patra[2,‡], Abha Choubey[1,¶] and Swati Jain[3,#]

[1]Department of Computer Science and Engineering,
Shri Shankaracharya Technical Campus, Bhilai (C. G.), India
[2]Department of Computer Science and Engineering,
Shri Shankaracharya Institute of Professional Management and Technology,
Raipur (C. G.), India
[3]Department of Computer Science, GJY Chhattisgarh College, Raipur (C. G.), India

Abstract

About seventy percent of the Indian population lives in villages or rural areas. Even after more than seventy years of Independence, rural India is lagging on the developmental index. So for the truth of development of India, the villages cannot be neglected rather the villages should be given special care. The Government of India is highly concerned about the development of rural India. Nowadays technology is playing a very important role in almost every walk of life. Accordingly, technology can be the real game changer for the development of rural India. Artificial Intelligence or AI, in short, is the future of the modern world and accordingly it has a lot for the development of rural India. This paper

---

* Corresponding Author's Email: someshdewangan2020@gmail.com.
† Corresponding Author's Email: sidd25876@gmail.com.
‡ Corresponding Author's Email: patra.jyotiprakash@gmail.com.
¶ Corresponding Author's Email: abha.is.shukla@gmail.com.
# Corresponding Author's Email: sjcscghed@gmail.com.

In: Applications of Artificial Intelligence in the Healthcare Sector
Editors: Jyoti Prakash Patra and Yogesh Kumar Rathore
ISBN: 979-8-88697-502-4

deals with the potential of Artificial Intelligence in the development of rural India.

Keywords: Indian population, rural India and development

2.1. Introduction

In the simplest of terms, Artificial Intelligence means to make the machine intelligent. In other words, the goal of Artificial Intelligence is to make the machine think like human beings. Hence Artificial Intelligence is also referred to as Machine Intelligence. Technically speaking Contrary to the natural intelligence exhibited by people and other animals, artificial intelligence, often known as machine intelligence, is intelligence demonstrated by machines. In computer science, the term "intelligent agent" refers to any device that can observe its environment and take activities to increase the likelihood that it will succeed in attaining its goals [1]. When a machine imitates "cognitive" abilities that people typically identify with other human minds, such as "learning" and "problem-solving," it is referred to as "artificial intelligence" [2]. Machine learning, computer vision, knowledge representation, expert systems, audio processing, and natural language processing are the core artificial intelligence technologies. A lot of research is being done now in the field of artificial intelligence, and it is showing promise. Health care, robotics, the military, agriculture, retail, manufacturing, game playing, the arts, banking & finance, the automobile, energy, and advertising are some of the notable application fields of artificial intelligence. The topic of rural development also holds great promise for artificial intelligence.

2.1.1. Rural Development

In the context of India, rural development is crucial. India is a sizable nation, and the majority of its citizens reside in the countryside or in villages. Without rural development, our nation cannot be regarded as developed. The population of rural areas is moving toward a better future for the cities as a result of urban development. The urban infrastructure is under a lot of stress as a result of this. To stop people from moving to metropolitan regions, the solution is to improve rural areas. The sole purpose of rural development is to raise the standard of living and economic standing of those who reside in rural areas. Exploitation has been the primary focus of rural development. However, the nature of rural areas has changed as a result of changes in global industrial networks and rising urbanization. Resource extraction and agriculture are increasingly being supplanted by specialist manufacturing, tourism, and leisure [3]. Instead of just encouraging agricultural or resource-based enterprises, rural towns now need to approach development from a wider viewpoint, which has increased focus on a variety of development goals. Rural region development depends on enterprise, education, physical infrastructure, and social infrastructure [4]. Due to its emphasis on locally created economic development techniques, rural development is also significant. Rural areas are highly different from one another, in contrast to metropolitan areas, which share many commonalities. As a result, there are several Different rural development strategies that are used globally in various regions. The phrase "rural development" is all-encompassing. Its primary concern is the growth of regions outside of the conventional metropolitan economic system.

2.1.2. What Is the Role of AI?

Technology and digitalization are seen as having a bright future thanks to artificial intelligence. As some of us are already aware, artificial intelligence refers to the process of giving robots human-like traits and the ability to think for themselves. There are several opportunities for governments and society to advance thanks to its ability to contribute to practically every industry sector. For this reason, numerous companies all over the world have implemented this technology into their practices, goods, and services.

Governments are now pursuing this technical advancement. They are currently attempting to deploy artificial intelligence in industries including healthcare, education, the economy, and agriculture as a result. Without a question, AI will form a crucial part of every nation's future. How will this technology affect industries like healthcare, though? How might it impact how individuals access medical care? AI, machine learning, and deep learning systems, for instance, can forecast patients' future outcomes. Doctors can identify and potentially prevent diseases in this manner while taking patients' vital signs.

2.1.3. Artificial Intelligence within the Healthcare System

Artificial intelligence (AI) helps in the field of healthcare in many ways, starting from clinical testing to disease identification and to helping doctors in decision making. There are so many medical institutes now collaborating with AI industries to make AI-based machinery as per their need. In a country like India, where the population is very high, the ratio of medical cases also higher than in other countries so they need assistance from machines to save time and to increase accuracy in disease prediction. However, their main issue is the growing population and the great number of issues that causes [5].

India suffers from a lot of healthcare issues as a result of its high population. Due to their poor infrastructure and lack of qualified medical professionals, they have very little access to services. Despite this, issues like this can be resolved with the use of artificial intelligence and technology. In this manner, the healthcare system could develop and produce better outcomes.

2.1.4. The Improvement of Rural Areas by AI

Agriculture is another industry, where artificial intelligence plays an important role. To feed the population, one needs to increase production, in such a scenario, AI is helping farmers in making decisions and to work with the latest tools. This development also includes other technologies like image identification, agricultural drones, plant monitoring system, and automated irrigation systems. The impact of AI on agriculture in nations with sizable rural populations, such as India, cannot be denied.

The high rates of school dropouts and the subpar quality of India's educational system are major problems as well. According to investigations, up to 50% of high school students in rural areas are unable to solve simple mathematics problems. By utilizing interactive learning, artificial intelligence may resolve problems like this. AI can assist in creating intelligent rural classrooms in this way to make learning more engaging for pupils. The modernization of classrooms in rural areas and their development are the key points of emphasis. All of this could result in higher educational standards in rural areas, giving the local community a better future.

2.1.5. Drone Operators

Drones are the eventual fate of horticulture. IoT and AI-empowered drones could assist with recognizing the different regions that need quick human consideration. Drone makers can utilize the rural population, train them and assist with dealing with the agribusiness drones. These drone administrators can assist with distinguishing irritations, flooding, dry season, and yield wastage.

2.1.6. Precision Animal Husbandry and Agriculture

Precision Agriculture or PA is seen that animal husbandry and agriculture are boosting the job market in rural India. PA can assist in finding the best mating seasons for numerous cattle and avian populations. The creation of milk, grain, eggs, meat, and leather can be developed dramatically with the consideration of Predictive science in cultivating and animal husbandry. Organizations like Intel, Google AI, IBM Watson, and Microsoft could assume a larger part in carrying PA to the focal point of the agricultural AI biological system.

2.1.7. Executives in Micro-Seeding Projects

Like micro-financing, we would discover no less than one-fifth of the country India populace is occupied with miniature cultivating projects. The leaders in micro-cultivating undertakings could come generally from the informed portion of the provincial populace who are essential science graduates. These science graduates could be prepared in government-subsidized AI IoT programs. Artificial intelligence and machine learning use cases in farming would open the work market for instructed youth with remunerating profession openings lined up with the country and Agri-based framework.

2.1.8. Farm Planning with Data Visualizers

Indian cultivating remains exceptionally unstructured, to a great extent because of the piece-land reservations. Deforestation, metropolitan disarray, and streamlined advances are add-ons to the list of difficulties. Data visualization organizations could utilize a huge piece of the country's populace who comprehend the homestead arranging guide better compared to other people. By utilizing robotics in agriculture and machine learning use cases in agriculture, we could see information perception turning into the middle stone of each homestead arranging project in India. Projects like Microsoft AI for Earth are a model. The rustic economy could be prepared to work with AI for Earth undertakings to evaluate the danger of dry season, flooding, and wildfire.

2.2. Literature Survey

2.2.1. Artificial Intelligence for Rural Development

The rural areas require three main things for their upliftment viz. Agriculture, Health, & Education and in all these three areas Artificial Intelligence has a lot to offer. The potential of Artificial Intelligence is provided as follows.

2.2.2. Artificial Intelligence in Agriculture

The primary line of work for those who reside in rural or village areas is agriculture. The level of living and quality of life of rural residents will automatically improve as agricultural productivity increases. Artificial Intelligence (AI) and Machine Learning (ML) are being rapidly adopted in agriculture for both agricultural goods and farming methods. In particular, cognitive computing, which is capable of understanding, learning, and reacting to various situations in order to boost efficiency, is well positioned to become the most significant technology in the agriculture industry. Giving all farmers in rural areas access to artificial intelligence-based services, such as chatbots and other conversational techniques, will enable them to keep up with and adopt new technologies. The primary areas where artificial intelligence will assist agriculture are listed in [6]:

- IoT-driven expansion
- production of insights via images
- Determining the best combination of agronomic products
- Crop health monitoring
- Irrigation automation methods that help farmers.

2.2.3. Artificial Intelligence in Education

Education is very important in the modern world. Education opens a lot of avenues for human beings. It is a well-known fact that the educational index of rural India is also poor. So education is to be delivered with the utmost priority. Artificial Intelligence is very helpful for educating the rural population as well. Artificial Intelligence can provide the following support in educating the rural people and benefitting them [7]:-Automating fundamental educational tasks like grading, evaluation, etc. is possible with artificial intelligence. The needs of the students can be catered for by educational software. AI-based technologies can identify areas in which courses need to be improved. AI tutors may provide additional support for learners. AI-driven systems may provide instructors and students with useful feedback, and they are changing how we locate and use information. Using AI Expert systems may alter teachers' responsibilities. AI can lessen the frightening nature of trial-and-error learning. How schools locate, educate, and assist kids may alter as a result of data powered by AI. AI could alter how kids learn, where they receive their education, and who instructs them.

2.2.4. Artificial Intelligence in Healthcare

The health index is likewise on the lower side in rural areas; hence urgent reform in the health sector is required. The application of algorithms and software to simulate human cognition in the processing of intricate medical data is known as artificial intelligence (AI) in healthcare. AI specifically refers to computer algorithms' capacity to make approximations of conclusions without direct human input. Analyzing correlations between prevention or treatment methods and patient outcomes is the main goal of health-related AI applications [8]. The health industry has found a number of artificial intelligence-based expert systems, such MYCIN, to be very useful. MYCIN is an extremely effective expert system for identifying diseases. Evidently, for the field of rural health, artificial intelligence may show to be a blessing [9].

The preservation of high-quality medical treatment is a global concern. There have been some corrective measures against metropolitan and semi-urban healthcare, of course, but there are still many problems with regard to rural health. One could argue that access to healthcare is a fundamental human right. Always being in excellent health is riches, which is essential to enjoyment and prosperity. Adds to the nation's economic development as well. Additionally, happy individuals are healthy people. In terms of creativity, happy people are productive [2]. In the IT industry, the healthcare sector is expanding quickly. The amount of data produced in the modern digital world is enormous, making it very challenging to store with a regular traditional database. Big Data can assist in addressing these issues in this situation for processing of enormous volumes of data. Big data is a term used to express the enormous scope of information. Data may be presented in an orderly or disorganized format [10].

Any association between improved tactical phases and decision production will follow data analytics [3]. Numerous uses for big data have been discovered in the healthcare sector. A few advantages of using big data in the healthcare industry include precise and accurate diagnosis, appropriate treatment choices, successful prevention planning, and quick and effective identification of a disease's underlying causes. Moreover, timely epidemiological forecast. The term "AI" is in vogue and as the globe moves closer to digitization, smartphone usage is rising quickly everywhere. The appropriate usage of a Smartphone can benefit us in a variety of ways. Smartphones now come with a variety of health-related apps, which promote better health. There are numerous mobile apps that help us keep track of our diet and weight. Giving people the information, they need to know about the health camps set up nearby via a Smartphone app is very beneficial for both individuals and governmental and nonprofit groups.

2.2.5. Application of Artificial Intelligence Technology in Agriculture

An Inter-Ministerial Committee looking into how to double farmers' incomes by 2022 have among other things, recognized the importance of digital technology in modernizing and organizing how rural India conducts its agricultural activities. Among the technologies are the Internet of Things (IoT), Big Data Analytics, Blockchain Technology, and Artificial Intelligence (AI). According to Union Minister for Agriculture & Farmers Welfare Narendra Singh Tomar in the Rajya Sabha, the use of new technologies including artificial intelligence and through gathering timely accurate information about crops, weather, and insects, farmers may increase crop productivity, and reduce the risk of crop loss.

Major technology interventions include:

- Creation of the mobile application Kisan Suvidha to make it easier for farmers to get information about crucial factors like the weather, market prices, plant protection, input dealers selling seeds, pesticides, and fertilizers, farm machinery, extreme weather alerts, soil health cards, cold storage facilities, and veterinary clinics and diagnostic labs. Farmers can become more aware of markets to sell their products, current market pricing, and market demand with the use of market intelligence. As a result, they may decide with knowing whether to sell produce at the appropriate time and price.
- Creation of the mobile application "Farm Machinery Package for Different Agro-Climatic Zones in India," which provides details on the farm machinery packages that are accessible by state, agro-climatic zone, district, cropping pattern, and power source.
- Creation of the "My Ciphet" mobile application to provide farmers with exact information about post-harvest equipment, goods, and technology produced by the Indian Council of Agriculture Research (ICAR).
- The ICAR has also assembled and posted on its website more than 100 mobile apps that were created by the ICAR, state agricultural universities (SAU), and Krishi Vigyan Kendras (KVKs). These mobile apps, which were created in the fields of agriculture, horticulture, veterinary medicine, dairy, poultry, fisheries, natural resource management, and integrated subjects, provide farmers with useful information about farming techniques, market prices for different commodities, weather-related data, advisory services, and other related topics.
- The creation of the mKisan Portal would allow enrolled farmers to receive SMS advisories on numerous crop-related topics.
- The e-National Agriculture Market (eNAM) initiative's debut, offers farmers a venue for electronic internet trading.
- The introduction of the Soil Health Card programme will help state governments provide soil health cards to all farmers nationwide once every two years. A soil health card informs farmers of the nutrient state of their soil and offers suggestions for the right amount of nutrients to apply to increase crop productivity and soil fertility.
- Applying machine learning techniques and other computer algorithms to categories crops and estimate crop areas.

Additionally, ICAR operates 684 Agricultural Technology Management Agencies (ATMAs) and 713 Krishi Vigyan Kendras (KVKs) at the district level to disseminate technologies to the farming community. Agri-clinics and Agri-Business Centers of entrepreneurs, agriculture fairs and exhibitions, the Kisan SMS site, focused publicity campaigns, agriculture fairs and exhibitions, and other methods are also employed to offer information to farmers, the minister continued.

Conclusion

Rural development is very important in today's scenario. It is important that every citizen of the country should be benefitted. For this, the development should not be limited to the urban parts only but also creep into the grassroots levels as well. From this paper, it is very clear that the field of Artificial Intelligence has a lot to offer for rural development. So the Government as well as other organizations should invest in Artificial Intelligence for the upliftment of rural areas. Many government agencies like ICAR, ATMA, and KVK are taking initiative to link the agriculture with latest technologies including artificial intelligence, the internet of things, robotics and drone technologies. Automated machines continuously come into the market to help the farmers in harvesting, monitoring the health of the plant, finding the proper fertilizer, and early detection of plant disease. Through this paper, we also found the need for a computer-aided design (CAD) system for plant disease detection, the need for small-size tractors that can work on small lands, and machinery which can be dissembled and assembled easily and easy carry for farmers of the village.

References

[1] Definition of AI as the study of intelligent agents: Poole, Mackworth & Goebel 1998, p. 1, which provides the version that is used in this article. Note that they use the term "computational intelligence" as a synonym for artificial intelligence. Russell & Norvig (2003) (who prefer the term "rational agent") and write "*The whole-agent view is now widely accepted in the field*" (Russell & Norvig 2003, p. 55).

[2] Russell, Peter Norvig. "*Artificial Intelligence: A Modern Approach by Stuart.*" Russell and Peter Norvig contributing writers, Ernest Davis... et al. (2010).

[3] Ward, Neil; Brown, David L. (1 December 2009). "Placing the Rural in Regional Development." *Regional Studies*. 43 (10): 1237– 1244. doi:10.1080/003434 00903234696.

[4] *Rural development research: a foundation for policy* (1. publ. ed.). Westport, Conn. [u.a.]: Greenwood Press. 1996. ISBN 0-313- 29726-6.

[5] Xiaoqi Lu, Yu Gu, Jianfeng Zhao, Ning Yu, Weitao Jia, "*Research and Implementation of Medical Information Format Conversion Based on Hl7 Version 2.X*," 10.1109/Csss.2011.5974909.

[6] https://www.mindtree.com/sites/default/files/2018-04/Artificial%20Intelligence %20in%20Agriculture.pdf seen on date 07th July 2022 at 02:00pm.

[7] https://www.teachthought.com/the-future-of-learning/10-roles-forartificial-intelligence-in-education/ seen on date 14th July 2022 at 09:00am.

[8] Coiera, E. (1997). *Guide to medical informatics, the Internet and telemedicine*. Chapman & Hall, Ltd.

[9] Lanhua Zhang, Xiaochen Xu, "*A Community Public Health System Design based on HL7 Criterions*," Vol. 4, No. 2; March 2011.

[10] Sanskruti Patel and Atul Patel," a big data revolution in health care sector: opportunities, challenges and technological advancements," *International Journal of Information Sciences and Techniques* (IJIST) Vol. 6, No.1/2, March 2016.

Chapter 3

An Artificial Intelligence-Based Pharmacy in Rural Areas

Preeti Tuli*, **Anand Tamrakar**† **and Abhishek Kumar Saw**‡
[1]Department of Computer Science and Engineering,
Shri Shankaracharya Institute of Professional Management and Technology,
Raipur (C.G.), India

Abstract

Artificial intelligence is drastically changing the world. It has changed and impacted the world on multiple levels and its effects have now reached rural areas. More than half of India's population live in rural areas and 58% of people's livelihood are based only on agriculture. The major issue people face in rural areas is in the field of healthcare.Medical facilities in rural areas are in serious need of advancement due to a lack of workers and an optimal environment. People in rural areas have to travel to towns and cities for disease diagnosis. This causes additional strain on their existing poor financial condition. Online doctor assistance using AI can provide consultation with doctors using phones. Health workers can be trained to operate an AI-based diagnosis and sampling system which provides reports of patients. It can also assemble, store and trace clinical data of individual patients. AI can also be used by doctors to develop personalized assessments. Early detection of diseases can prevent lives. Prediction methodology and algorithms are advancing and providing precise output based on records of patients. During Covid-19,

* Corresponding Author's Email: p.tuli@ssipmt.com.
† Corresponding Author's Email: a.tamrakar@ssipmt.com.
‡ Corresponding Author's Email: ak.saw@ssipmt.com.

In: Applications of Artificial Intelligence in the Healthcare Sector
Editors: Jyoti Prakash Patra and Yogesh Kumar Rathore
ISBN: 979-8-88697-502-4

AI played a major role in tracking and predicting morbidity and mortality rate. It was also used for monitoring cases, predicting future outbreaks, and pattern recognition for studying disease trends.AI-based robots are used to help patients in hospitals during a pandemic. Artificial intelligence can help the advancement of healthcare facilities in rural areas.

Keywords: health care centers, health care facilities, health insurance, Primary Health Care (PHC)

3.1. Introduction

In the past few years, Artificial Intelligence has changed many sectors, especially in machine learning and deep learning. Artificial Intelligence is a very rapidly growing technology all over the fields like home automation, self-driving cars, and many more. Some examples are facing recognition, image recognition, etc. With the help of AI, we can improve professional work and clinical efficiency and reduces medical errors. In most developed countries, this type of technique is used widely. At the time of surgery if the doctors are unable to do minute surgery like intestine, brain neurons, etc. so the robotic arm with AI-implemented technology can work effortlessly.

In the field of medical healthcare, AI was first implemented as a medical diagnosis decision support system (MDDS). In the early 1990s, AI was already introduced, when physicians, doctors, and surgeons made their improvement in the diagnosis technique with the help of computer-aided programs,There are so many modern technologies available now like modern computers with high-speed processors and large amounts of data which are very helpful to understand and analyze. There are several AI applications in the medical field such as clinical, diagnosis, rehabilitation, surgical, and other medical practices. AI applications deal with a large amount of data related to the medical field like new diseases, prevention, and treatment.

AI applications in the medical field will help doctors in many ways. Automatic machines like digital medical imaging, CT scans, sonography, and many more machines. Through AI technology high-resolution images of body parts can be obtained very accurately and very quickly. In the past, doctors needed a lot of training and time to diagnose a patient (for critical cases sometimes it might take several days). After diagnosing for hours and days, the doctor will get an accurate result or actual problem. For gaining experience he/she needs to diagnose hundreds of patients but now with the help of AI technology doctors or specialists need a few minutes or hardly 1-2 hours. In many developed countries and also in developing countries, new doctors or practitioners have to study computer science subjects, or at least they know how to work with AI-driven technology. It saves so much time for newcomers. There are many apps and platforms already available that help in computer-assisted diagnostics (Human DX app).

Scientists have not only made devices for doctors but also make devices for normal people and patients. Scientists made wearable devices that help people to check their pulse rate or heart rate. Today's smart watches and smart phones have a feature that can detect our pulse rate, heart rate, calories burned during heavy work or exercises, and many more. The recently launched smart watch has a feature that if any patient whose heart rate is in an abnormal state, their heartbeat detectors or EKG machines on their watch or cell phone directly contact their respective doctors or his/her close relatives. Pacemakers and Implantable Cardioverter Defibrillators these devices are also developed by scientists so that a heart failure person can be able to live life normally.

3.2. Literature Survey

As we all know health is the most important aspect for all living beings. Developed countries and their governments gave free medical checkups for all and also used various techniques for detecting diseases and doing operations with the help of AI-based technology. But in developing countries, medical facilities are not provided properly or due to a shortage of medicines and instruments, people may die. In developing countries healthcare is quite poor, the major cause is the large population and people below the poverty line. Low literacy rate, poverty, inadequate monitoring of patients, and many other issues face in rural areas.

Simultaneously, the need for cost-effective and timely healthcare has risen dramatically as a result of exponential population expansion and limited financial resources [1]. In addition, the government, financial institutions, and hospitals must pay close attention to the rapid increase in communicable and lifestyle diseases [2]. The Indian healthcare industry, particularly in rural areas, is suffering from a severe shortage of drugs and personnel [3]. Various policies, such as incentives, regulatory impediments, and funding sources, influence the availability of employees in rural areas [4].

Furthermore, the impact of medical tourism has been discussed, with the conclusion that international healthcare collaboration, medical insurance coverage, and information system are dependent factors, whereas the medical tourism market, pharmaceutical science research, and medical and paramedical staffs are independent factors [5]. To interpret the supply chain and patient arrival rates, a Model was established to identify the components that directly influence the inventory management and supply chain in a Hospital which is known as the Interpretive Structural Model (ISM) [6].Other aspects of healthcare that have been examined so far also contribute to the corpus of knowledge.

Several causes are responsible for infant mortality in rural areas, including water-borne infections, infectious diseases, malnutrition, and an unsanitary environment, all of which are exacerbated by poor rural healthcare. Malaria, filaria, and kala-azar are among the more challenging infections to treat. According to a report, more than 85% of rural children are suffering from malnutrition. According to the NFHS-III, India's IMR was 57 per thousand live births [7].

The lack of utilization of human-made resources at different levels causes the rural health system to run inefficiently. As a result, provisions must be made for upgrading the existing rural health system based on an examination of the system's deficiencies.

3.3. Problem Statement

India has a multi-stage, incredibly intricate healthcare system. Even though such systems are entirely the responsibility of the government, village-level management is essential to their efficiency. Additionally crucial are several supply chain, financial, social, and environmental issues. For rural healthcare to operate effectively, facilitators and impediments must be interrelated. Due to a lack of knowledge about key system drivers and dependent components, government policymakers are unsure of the long-term policy results under various barriers. Rural healthcare systems thus confront a range of issues and challenges, such as a lack of human resources, inadequate building infrastructure, poor disease/illness forecasting, a shortage of essential medications, and a lack of coordination.Therefore, it is necessary to identify the interrelationships and hierarchical levels of these components to support the health policymakers in managing the system's performance.

3.4. Challenges for Rural Health System: An Overview

Instead of being the outcome of a single incident, the health system's poor performance in rural areas is the product of a coordinated expansion of a failing system. It indicates not only shortcomings in current infrastructure and policies but also a roadblock to further advancement. Public health expenses have been disregarded by the state and the general populace. The majority of people believe that public health spending is wasteful.

They think that the standard of treatment and medications at government-run hospitals has declined.

India's public health system has been affected by its growing investment in private physicians and hospitals. Poor people are turning to the commercial sector for assistance due to their frustration and disillusionment with the government's growing inefficiency, which forces them to take out expensive loans or abandon them to the whims of "quacks." Therefore, we must look at the root causes of India's public health system's collapse.

3.4.1. Underutilization of Existing Rural Hospitals

In rural areas, effective health infrastructure is lacking; on the other hand, this infrastructure is underutilized. Rural patients frequently avoid local rural hospitals despite equal medical treatment being available. According to Chilimuntha, Anil K., Kumudini R. Thakor, and Jeremiah S. Mulpuri [8], hospital factors (size, ownership, and distance) and patient characteristics (payment source, medical condition, age, and race) influence the choice between rural hospitals and urban hospitals. Rural inhabitants think that any hospitalization can be handled at urban facilities.

Consequently, rural hospitals are either closed or open but without patients. Due to the lack of all-season roads, access in many locations is dependent on the weather [8]. The facility closes as a result of widespread service absenteeism. Public doctors frequently provide private treatments rather than traveling to their authorized centers. [9].

3.4.2. Inadequate Human Resources

The results of the survey show that primary healthcare providers in India have an absence rate of about 40%. [10].

For a whole year, frequent weekday visits were made to 143 public facilities in India as part of this study. In basic healthcare institutions, over 45% of doctors were absent [10]. The percentage of nurses who miss work varies from 27% in Madhya Pradesh to more than 50% in Bihar, Karnataka, Uttarakhand, and Uttar Pradesh.

A major absence of adequate administrative effort to provide high-quality services may be the cause of this high absence rate.

3.4.3. Lack of Community Participation

The needs of the rural population are largely unmet by the public health system, particularly in rural areas. A pandemic has resulted from the disregard for community pleas for the treatment, diagnosis, and prevention of several diseases. Ineffective disease surveillance, hygiene maintenance, and sanitization are the results of not consulting the local communities. The pandemic spreads as a result of a lack of contact between medical personnel and the local population. Communities must to be involved in the development, administration, and management of neighborhood primary healthcare facilities as well as other types of support.

3.4.4. Remedies in Rural Health System

The issue of rural health has been addressed using a variety of strategies and missions. To formally establish the current rural health structure, the government has undertaken a variety of efforts.

3.4.5. National Rural Health Mission (NRHM)

One of the most important developments in rural health is the National Rural Health Mission (NRHM). It was founded in 2005 to treat ailments and challenges in basic healthcare, as well as to enhance the health system and the state of rural inhabitants' health. Following the Millennium Development Goals and broad principles outlined in national and state health policies, it provides all people with healthcare that is easily accessible, affordable, effective, responsible, and reliable, with a focus on the most vulnerable and poorest segments of the population.

NRHM, a federal government flagship program, aims to increase access to essential healthcare services in rural areas of India by making architectural corrections to the current healthcare delivery system and promoting better nutrition, sanitation, cleanliness, and access to safe drinking water. Under the NHRM, several actions have been done to upgrade the state of the deteriorating infrastructure in rural health care.

The NRHM has strengthened the healthcare facilities that operate at the unit level, including PHC and SC. Numerous PHCs have been upgraded to 24-hour PHCs with sufficient medical care.

Through a statewide network of ASHA employees, patients have also been connected to the traditional healthcare system.

3.4.6. Janani Suraksha Yojana (JSY)

The National Rural Health Mission (NRHM flagship)'s program, Janani Suraksha Yojana, was created by the Indian government to improve institutional delivery and reduce maternal and newborn mortality. Giving birth at a governmental or privately authorized medical institution is compensated for mothers. Employees of the rural JSY increase the number of institutional deliveries by escorting expectant women to the most suitable healthcare facilities for prenatal care. They act as a conduit between the public and the rural health system. The Development Research Services (DRS) of UNFPA found that in 2008, 73 percent of births in the Indian states of Madhya Pradesh and Orissa took place in a medical institution.

ASHAs recommended having their babies in a hospital to 91% of moms in Orissa, 84% in Uttar Pradesh, 74% in Bihar, and 72% in Rajasthan (64 percent). Except for Bihar, where it was only slightly lower at 85%, more than 90% of mothers stated that their pregnancies were registered throughout the ANC period [11].

3.4.7. Mobile-Based Primary Health Care System

The mobile-based primary health care system is essential to the field of rural health. Primary healthcare is now more easily accessible because of mobile-based services [12]. This mobile healthcare system, first debuted in 2005, communicates a person's vital signs using a cell phone. All over the nation, medical professionals may be able to remotely monitor patients with chronic diseases. This entails offering a wide range of services, including vaccination, disease prevention, basic sanitation, nutrition promotion, health education, and proper illness and injury care [13].The case is being spearheaded by the Centre for Development of Advanced Computing, a business based in Bangalore (CDAC). Among the software components under development are patient database management, doctor-patient communication, medical data collection (ECG, images of the heart, lung, and eye, for example), and scheduling management. A central repository of the Primary Health Center management system with a Web interface is being proposed as an open-source database. By providing a translation interface, it also develops localization support for mobiles in native and other Indian languages.

3.5. The Application of Medical Artificial Intelligence Technology in Rural Areas of Developing Countries

Artificial intelligence (AI), a fast-evolving branch of computer science, is now being actively applied in the medical industry to enhance clinical work's professionalism and effectiveness while also reducing the risk of medical errors. The disparity in access to healthcare between urban and rural areas is a critical issue in developing nations, and the lack of skilled healthcare professionals is a major factor in the unavailability and poor quality of healthcare in rural areas. According to several studies, using AI or computer-assisted medical approaches could lead to better healthcare outcomes in developing nations' rural areas. Therefore, it is worthwhile to discuss and investigate the creation of medical AI technology that is appropriate for rural locations.

Artificial intelligence techniques not only can predict the disease but also may provide suggestions to the professional based on training. The same may be help individuals to decide in the absence of professionals. This article suggests a multilayer network of medical AI service providers, encompassing a national medical AI development center, regional medical AI support centers, and frontline medical AI systems (basic level) (top-level).

3.6. The Prospect of Medical AI Technology

3.6.1. AI in Personalized Medicine

In a new healthcare paradigm known as personalized medicine (precision medicine), diseases are treated and prevented depending on the unique conditions of each patient, including their genetic makeup, psychosocial makeup, environment, and way of life. The massive amount of data generated by all of this information can only be processed and integrated by AI technology. According to Mesko, "AI is essential to precision medicine."For instance, Deep Variant, created by Google, Inc., is a very accurate deep neural network-based genetic analysis system.

3.6.2. AI in Healthcare System Management

Treatment-based care is the main focus of current healthcare systems, which makes them unable to offer suitable low-cost interaction for healthy high-risk clients. At the same time, the global economic toll brought on by the chronic disease epidemic is significant. To lower rising healthcare costs and enhance healthcare outcomes, the government in the United States is thinking about integrating AI personal health monitoring platforms into healthcare management systems.The American National Institutes of Health has financed the development of the Smartphone app AiCure, which keeps track of patients' ailments and prescriptions.

3.6.3. Medical Robots with AI

Assistive medical robots and equipment are also among the applications of artificial intelligence in medicine. Tele robots, for instance, can help in the interaction of patients with the doctor; assist handicapped persons while walking, standing, or sitting; and also can help them to communicate with other patients/doctors. Additionally, robots can serve as assistant surgeons during operations. One of the most popular robotic surgical systems is the da Vinci Surgical System; over 3400 units had been utilized as of 2015.

3.6.4. AI in Pharma Industry

Artificial intelligence has been used in many pharmacy industries and its fields such as drug discovery, drug formulation, and polypharmacology as well to increase productivity and improve the efficiency of drugs. In the pharmacy industry, AI is used in many ways such as drug components analysis, drug life cycle analysis, and to perform many clinical tests [14]. In rural areas, many pharmaceutical products like automated sugar and health monitoring system help villagers to diagnose and save their lives.

Conclusion

The rural health sector in India is one of the country's most important development issues. It has, nevertheless, been a neglected sector of the Indian economy. Since the country's public health condition is so dire right now, any effort to improve it will almost probably require administrative measures. To ensure a strong direct or indirect relationship between these factors and health, these administrative measures also include public health regulation and enforcement, human resource development and capacity building, population stabilization, and the enhancement of disease surveillance technology. Strong surveillance systems will support monitoring and policy development. Health professionals' ability to manage and lead will be facilitated by the public health sector's strong human resources. There has been a lack of both physical infrastructure and human resources in rural healthcare. Even though the positions have government approval, many of them remain vacant. The state of rural health has gotten worse due to medical professionals' general apathy. Many people living in rural areas are unable to receive treatment for basic illnesses, either because there are no healthcare facilities nearby or because they cannot afford to travel there. The top-down approach is used in many departments. One of the most striking effects of this top-down approach has been the failure of the majority of State-supported community health worker schemes.

Therefore, we must redesign the current rural health system both architecturally and operationally to incorporate the advancement of AI-enabled facilities to improve the overall rural health sector. In the pharmaceutical industry, AI is applied to manage the database, process the clinical data, and predict the possibility of disease based on historical data, still, there is a need for AI in the field of drug discovery, in identifying the drug components, identifying protein structure, and drug compounds.

References

[1] Kumar Dinesh. "India's rural healthcare systems: structural modeling." *International Journal of Health Care Quality Assurance*, (2018).

[2] Gangolli Leena, Duggal Ravi and Shukla Abhay. (2005). *Review of Healthcare In India*.

[3] Nardi DA, Gyurko CC. The global nursing faculty shortage: Status and solutions for change. *J NursScholarsh,* 2013 Sep;45(3):317-26. doi: 10.1111/jnu.12030. Epub 2013 Apr 5. PMID: 23895289.

[4] Figueroa, M., Upadhyaya, N. M., Sperschneider, J., Park, R. F., Szabo, L. J., Steffenson, B., & Dodds, P. N. (2016). Changing the game: using integrative genomics to probe virulence mechanisms of the stem rust pathogen Puccinia graminis f. sp. tritici. *Frontiers in Plant Science*, 7, 205.

[5] Bikash Ranjan Debata, Bhaswati Patnaik, Mahapatra SS, Sreekumar S. 2013."Efficiency measurement amongst medical tourism service providers in India," *International Journal for ResponsibleTourism, FundatiaAmfiteatru,* vol. 1(1), pages 24-31.

[6] Kumar D. "India's rural healthcare systems: structural modeling." *International Journal of Health Care Quality Assurance*, 31, no. 7 (2018): 757-774.

[7] Shreekant Iyengar and Ravindra H Dholakia. "*Access of the Rural Poor to Primary Healthcare in India.*" (2011): 03.

[8] Jaysawal, Dr. "Rural health system in India: A review." *International Journal of Social Work and Human Services Practice*, (2015): 29-37.

[9] Bhandari Laveesh and SiddharthaDutta. "Health infrastructure in rural India." *India infrastructure report,* 2007 (2007): 265-85.

[10] Chaudhury Nazmul, Hammer J, Kremer M, Muralidharan K and Halsey Rogers F. 2006. "Missing in Action: Teacher and health worker Absence in Developing Countries." *Journal of Economic Perspectives*, 20 (1): 91-116.

[11] Jaysawal, Dr. "Rural health system in India: A review." *International Journal of Social Work and Human Ramana.* "Mobile based primary health care system for rural India." In *W3C workshop on Role of Mobile Technologies Services Practice*, (2015): 29-37.

[12] Murthy MV. in *Fostering Social Development*, vol. 17, pp. 1-8. 2008.

[13] Rahar Upendra Singh. "Mobile based primary health care system for rural India." *International Journal of Nursing Education*, 3 (2011): 61-63.

[14] Henstock Peter V. "Artificial intelligence for pharma: time for internal investment." *Trends in pharmacological sciences*, 40, no. 8 (2019): 543-546.

Chapter 4

FW-MCDM: Feature Weighted Multi-Criteria Decision-Making Techniques for Multi-Label Feature Selections

Gurudatta Verma[1,*] and Sunil Kumar Dewangan[2,†]
[1]Department of Information Technology, National Institute of Technology, Raipur (C.G.), India
[2]Department of Computer Science and Engineering, Shri Shankaracharya Institute of Professional Management and Technology, Raipur (C.G.), India

Abstract

Data collected from different sources are high dimensional in nature and contain an enormous number of attributes, which degrades the performance of classification and increases the storage cost of data. It becomes very difficult when data is multi-label (ML) in which one sample belongs to more than one class. So, feature selection (FS) is essential for ML data to reduce relevance and redundancy among features and labels. In this paper, we propose a FS selection technique for ML data, Feature Weighted Multi-Criteria Decision Making (FW-MCDM) method which is a filter technique. In the first step feature, the weighting technique is applied to obtain relevant features from ML data. Further reduced features are adopted by TOPSIS to rank the features for feature subset selection. The novelty of the proposed FW-MCDM technique was calibrated in the experimental section using MLKNN classifier over different benchmark datasets and achieved significant improvement in the classification accuracy and average precision.

* Corresponding Author's Email: gverma.phd2021.it@nitrr.ac.in.
† Corresponding Author's Email: s.dewangan@ssipmt.com.

In: Applications of Artificial Intelligence in the Healthcare Sector
Editors: Jyoti Prakash Patra and Yogesh Kumar Rathore
ISBN: 979-8-88697-502-4

Keywords: MCDM, MLKNN, multi-label classification, feature selection, feature weighting

4.1. Introduction

The problem in the real world mostly consists of the huge amount of data, getting useful information, and storage of data becomes very multifaceted. Collected data from various sources are very high dimensional and contain a substantial number of features or attributes. The dataset contains different features that are not always valuable for mining, some of them are immaterial, and inessential which may reduce the performance of the prediction model.

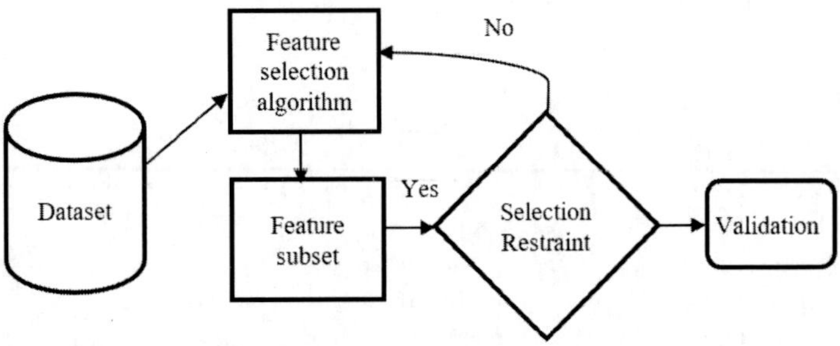

Figure 4.1. Feature selection process.

Henceforth selecting the most relevant feature from the dataset by keeping an eye on preserving the accuracy of the model is essential for the feature selection problem. Feature selection can be defined as it is the process of choosing an optimal subset of features according to certain criteria, the overall feature selection process can be described in figure 4.1. If a dataset contains M number of features, then 2^M subsets are possible from which optimal subset must be picked, an optimal feature subset is the smallest subset, which maximizes the classification accuracy finding the smallest subset is the NP-hard problem, the size of search space increases as a number of features in the dataset, to handle such problem numerous methodologies have been proposed. Comprehensive search, greedy search, random search etc. are the techniques applied to function selection problems to locate the best subset. Many methods are plagued by premature convergence, vast complexity, and elevated computational cost. For this reason, met heuristic algorithms get so much attention to deal with this type of condition.

A machine learning approach called "Multi-label learning" is used to learn from multi-label data, where every instance connected multi-labels. A major difference between multi-label learning and traditional binary or multi-class learning is that the labels in multi-label learning are not mutually exclusive, suggesting that each instance may be relevant to multiple labels. Thus, one of the major challenges with multi-label learning is how to develop the correlations with different labels efficiently. In comparison with binary label matching it becomes more critical. In the following, we describe some fundamental challenges in the successful application of multi-label learning in real-world problems.

- The first challenge is how to build an effective relationship between multi-labels to increase classification accuracy. Unlike binary labels, in multi-label learning, the labels are correlated with each other, so there will always be a challenge of how to measure the strength of correlations in the label space for improved prediction is crucial.
- The second challenge of multi-label learning lies in the class imbalance problem. When each label is treated independently, in most cases instances are unrelated to a particular label. That's why each label has less number of positive instances and more number of negative instances, which generates data imbalance. So, in such a case, it is difficult to design a well-accurate classifier for these labels without considering the label correlations.
- The third challenge is concerned with the effectiveness and efficiency of multi-label learning for large-scale problems, especially when both the data dimensionality and the quantity of labels are huge. Multi-label learning also suffers from the curse of dimensionality, and many existing multi-label learning methods are less effective for high-dimensional data since data points become sparse and far away from each other in high-dimensional space.

Here we are focusing on the problem of the curse of dimensionality in multi-label learning. In this chapter, we have proposed the use of the feature-weighted multi-criterion decision-making (MCDM) approach for feature selection to improvise the performance of multi-label classification. Our key contributions are:

- To solve the class imbalance problem in multi-label data we have proposed to use of KNN-based feature weighting.
- KNN-based feature weight passed to Technique of Order Preference by Similarity to Ideal Solution (TOPSIS), as a decision matrix for ranking of features.
- To prove its superiority proposed technique has been tested on 5 benchmark datasets.

The rest of the chapter is organized as: In the next section some related work has been discussed, the methodology is discussed in the next section, and in section IV experimental results are shown. Finally, the chapter is concluded, and the future scope is discussed.

4.2. Literature Survey

4.2.1. Multi-Label Learning

In the multi-label data, each instance has its own weightage associated with multi-label, to deal with such complex data structure a machine learning technique is used called Multi-label learning. There is a difference between traditional binary label learning and multi-label learning, in which labels are not independent like binary learning. It means in such learning, each instance may correlate with multiple labels at the same time. Thus, one of the key challenges of multi-label learning is how to exploit the correlations among different labels effectively. Table 4.1 shows the dataset structure of the multi-label dataset, where X is the feature set with M number of features and Y is the label set with L labels.

Table 4.1. Multilabel dataset structure

X (Attributes)				Y (Labels)			
X(1)	X(1)	....	X(M)	Y(1)	Y(2)	....	Y(L)
X(11)	X(12)	....	X(1M)	0	1	....	0
X(21)	X(22)	....	X(2M)	1	0	....	0
....	....	....	....	....	....	....	....
X(N1)	X(N2)	....	X(NM)	0	1	....	1

From the table, we can say that the dimensionality of multi-label data is high. One of the major issues in high-dimension data analysis is called the curse of dimensionality. The curse of dimensionality intends that for given sample size, there are the highest amount of features above which the performance of an algorithm will reduce rather than improve. Dimensionality reduction, which extracts a small number of features by removing irrelevant, redundant, and noisy information, is an effective way to mitigate the curse of dimensionality. Dimensionality reduction has been widely used in many domains for data compression, noise removal, etc. It leads to a significant reduction of the size of the data while some important properties of the original data set are preserved.

4.2.2. Background Study

Shina Kashef et al. By. [1] suggested filtering using the concept of Pareto-dominance in selecting features for multiple labels. For the relationship between features and labels, the condition of consistency symmetrical uncertainty (SU) is applied. Newton Spolaôr et al. [2] proposed Label Construction for Feature selection (LCFS) method, which creates new binary variables based on label relation that is added as a new label with the original dataset to augment the information for feature selection. Wanfu Gao et al. [3] proposed a filter-based method named Dynamic Change of Selected Feature with the class (DCSF) that presents a new term based on the relevancy of the dynamic changed information between the label and selected feature. Jaesung Lee et al. [4] proposed a method for identifying efficient score functions for a multi-label feature by removing nonessential functions from entropy calculation. Jaesung Lee et al. [5] proposed multi-label feature selection criterion based on mutual information that selection feature subsets by boosting relevancy between classes and features. Jun Huang et al. [6] proposed feature selection method Label-Specific features for multi-label classification with Missing Labels (LSML) for incomplete training data with missing labels. The high-order label correlation learning has been done to augment new supplementary labels for recovery and feature-specific learning has been done. Zhi-FenHe et al. [7] joint learning framework of multi-Label classification and label correlations with Missing labels and Feature selection (MLMF) that transform the multi-label training data into single binary variables, then the sparse features are selected using l2,1-norms. Rui Huang et al. [8] proposed a filter method, manifold-based constraint Laplacian score (MCLS) that transforms the logical labels into numerical labels using manifold to impose the numerical label as like-mindedness between the training sample and the relevancy of the features are determined by the numerical and local properties of data. Jaesung Lee et al. [9] proposed a memetic algorithm to refine the feature subset generated by genetic algorithm (GA) by removing the redundant and irrelevant features and adding relevant features to improve the muti-label classification precision and speed. Hyunki Lim et al. [10] proposed a wrapper method for multi-label feature selection based on an evolutionary algorithm (EA) that generates the initial population by considering the relevancy between the feature and the labels.

4.3. Methodology

Amin Hashemi [11] has used TOPSIS as a feature selection technique for multi-label classification. In this research, we have proposed the use of modified TOPSIS to improve the performance of the TOPSIS technique for getting an efficient feature ranking called FW-MCDM. Here FW means feature weight using the KNN algorithm and MCDM means multi-criterion decision-making technique which is TOPSIS. Use of KNN is used to overcome class imbalance problems in the multi-label dataset. Figure 4.2 shows the workflow of the proposed approach FW-MCDM. FW-MCDM has been tested on a well-known MLKNN classification algorithm.

4.3.1. Feature Weighting (KNN)

Input: Feature Set
Output: Feature weight

1. For each number of features M
2. Calculate Euclidian distance between instance and feature
3. Calculate neighbor with k=5
4. End loop step 1
5. Calculate the Distance between one instance and its neighbor as WdY
6. Calculate feature weight using WdY

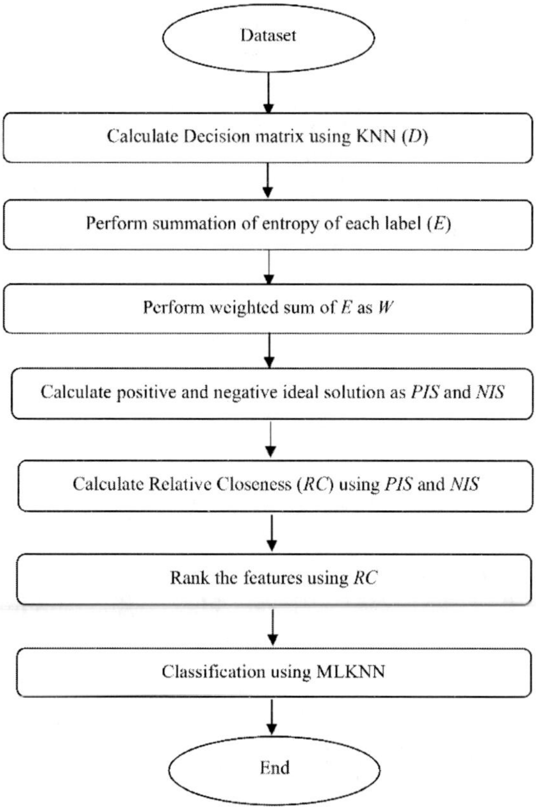

Figure 4.2. Proposed workflow.

4.4. Result and Discussion

To prove the superiority of FW-MCDM, it has been tested on 4 benchmark datasets as described in Table 4.2. Dataset download from a public repository of multi-label data Mulan.

Table 4.2. Dataset description

Dataset	Samples	Features	Label	Domain
Corel5k	5000	499	374	images
Enron	1702	1001	53	Text
Medical	978	1449	45	Text
Sence	2407	294	6	image

4.4.1. Multi-Label Learning Evaluation Parameters

Let T = {(xi, Yi) :i = 1, . . . , n} be a given test set, and h be the multi-label classifier, where Yi ⊆ L is a correct label subset and L = {lj: j = 1, . . . , q} is the set of all labels. Given an instance xi, a set of labels predicted by a multi-label classifier denoted as Zi, and f (·, ·) as a real-valued function which is returned by most multi-label learning systems.

- *Hamming Loss:* Hamming Loss (HL) measures the number of times that an instance–label pair is classified wrong.

$$\text{Hamming} - Loss(h,T) = \frac{1}{n}\sum_{i=1}^{n} \frac{|Y_i \Delta Z_i|}{|L|} \tag{4.1}$$

where Δ stands for the symmetric difference between two sets

- *Ranking Loss:* Ranking Loss (RL) evaluates the number of reversely ordered label pairs, an irrelevant label is ranked higher than a relevant label.

$$rloss\ (f) = \frac{1}{n}\sum_{i=1}^{n} \frac{1}{|Y_i||\bar{Y}_i|} \mid \{(y',y'') \mid f(x_i,y') \leq f(x_i,y''), (y',y'') \in Y_i \times \bar{Y}_i\} \mid \tag{4.2}$$

- *One error:* One Error (OE) evaluates how many times the top-ranked label is not relevant to the set of labels of the instance.

$$\text{One - Error}\ (f) = \frac{1}{n}\sum_{i=1}^{n} \left\| \left[\underset{y \in Y_i}{arg\,max} \{f(x_i,y)\} \right] \notin Y_i \right\| \tag{4.3}$$

- *Average precision:* Average Precision (AP) evaluates the average percentage of relevant labels ranked higher than an actual label y ∈ Yi.

$$Avg - Pre\ (f) = \frac{1}{n}\sum_{i=1}^{n} \frac{1}{|Y_i|} \times \sum_{y \in Y_i} \frac{\{y' | rank_f\ (x,y') \leq rank_f\ (x_i,y), y' \in Y_i\}}{rank_f(x_i,y)} \tag{4.4}$$

- *Coverage*: It evaluates the average number of steps that are needed to go down in the list of ranked labels to cover all the relevant labels of the instance.

$$\text{coverage}\ (f) = \frac{1}{n}\sum_{i=1}^{n} \max_{y \in Y_i} rank_f(x_i, y) - 1 \qquad (4.5)$$

4.4.2. Experiment

Table 4.3-4.8 describes the comparison of the well-known algorithm MFS-MCDM [11] and the proposed method (FW-MCDM) based on different evaluation parameters as discussed in section 4.1.

From the different tables, we can conclude that the proposed technique FW-MCDM performs well over the MCDM technique.

Table 4.3. Accuracy over 10/20/30/40 feature subset

Dataset	No. of Feature	Accuracy	
		MFS-MCDM [11]	FW-MCDM
corel5k	10	0.011042	0.011439
	20	0.014683	0.014150
	30	0.020575	0.021408
	40	0.022317	0.023026
Enron	10	0.351890	0.347220
	20	0.354830	0.375830
	30	0.372610	0.387240
	40	0.330680	0.409330
Medical	10	0.578430	0.290280
	20	0.675620	0.689550
	30	0.692670	0.695240
	40	0.637250	0.686700
Scene	10	0.188150	0.301280
	20	0.333330	0.512820
	30	0.476090	0.537600
	40	0.495840	0.579180
Ranking	W|T|L	3|0|16	16|0|3

Table 4.4. Hamming loss over 10/20/30/40 feature subset

Dataset	No. of Feature	Hamming Loss	
		MFS-MCDM [11]	FW-MCDM
corel5k	10	0.009372	0.009320
	20	0.009513	0.009352
	30	0.009393	0.009358
	40	0.009414	0.009326
Enron	10	0.053552	0.052553
	20	0.054606	0.052248
	30	0.051998	0.050139
	40	0.052913	0.048613
Medical	10	0.014038	0.021427
	20	0.012958	0.012868
	30	0.011367	0.011260
	40	0.012845	0.012333
Scene	10	0.158700	0.150730
	20	0.144140	0.120760
	30	0.125430	0.110880
	40	0.119370	0.106200
Ranking	W|T|L	1|0|15	15|0|1

Table 4.5. Ranking loss over 10/20/30/40 feature subset

Dataset	No. of Feature	Ranking Loss	
		MFS-MCDM [11]	FW-MCDM
corel5k	10	0.148430	0.139850
	20	0.138890	0.138110
	30	0.141870	0.137430
	40	0.138320	0.136290
Enron	10	0.098710	0.095609
	20	0.099538	0.094013
	30	0.097476	0.090185
	40	0.093669	0.088187
Medical	10	0.062660	0.071257
	20	0.047092	0.041294
	30	0.033050	0.035037
	40	0.046122	0.033154
Scene	10	0.241420	0.182330
	20	0.168040	0.127080
	30	0.145300	0.110190
	40	0.118220	0.098623
Ranking	W|T|L	2|0|14	14|0|2

Table 4.6. One error over 10/20/30/40 feature subset

Dataset	No. of Feature	One Error	
		MFS-MCDM [11]	FW-MCDM
corel5k	10	0.766500	0.750000
	20	0.739000	0.743000
	30	0.751500	0.738500
	40	0.715500	0.720500
Enron	10	0.295590	0.288240
	20	0.308820	0.276470
	30	0.279410	0.244120
	40	0.283820	0.258820
Medical	10	0.322250	0.473150
	20	0.209720	0.227620
	30	0.196930	0.186700
	40	0.189260	0.186700
Scene	10	0.543660	0.474010
	20	0.411640	0.350310
	30	0.402290	0.314970
	40	0.324320	0.290020
Ranking	W|T|L	4|0|12	12|0|4

Table 4.7. Coverage over 10/20/30/40 feature subset

Dataset	No. of Feature	Coverage	
		MFS-MCDM [11]	FW-MCDM
corel5k	10	120.40	117.27
	20	118.08	116.58
	30	119.26	116.57
	40	116.63	116.04
Enron	10	13.90	13.54
	20	14.30	13.13
	30	14.21	12.95
	40	13.45	12.72
Medical	10	3.57	3.89
	20	3.08	2.62
	30	2.13	2.35
	40	2.96	2.07
Scene	10	1.29	0.98
	20	0.93	0.70
	30	0.80	0.62
	40	0.67	0.56
Ranking	W|T|L	2|0|14	14|0|2

Table 4.8. Average precision over 10/20/30/40 feature subset

Dataset	No. of Feature	Average Precision	
		MFS-MCDM [11]	FW-MCDM
corel5k	10	0.21154	0.31535
	20	0.22946	0.31776
	30	0.22798	0.31808
	40	0.24133	0.32311
Enron	10	0.62237	0.70160
	20	0.62522	0.71175
	30	0.64201	0.72266
	40	0.64199	0.74016
Medical	10	0.73869	0.70260
	20	0.82629	0.84035
	30	0.85266	0.85682
	40	0.84802	0.88460
Scene	10	0.64929	0.72285
	20	0.74269	0.81634
	30	0.75800	0.85859
	40	0.80287	0.88156
Ranking	W|T|L	1|0|15	15|0|1

Conclusion

In this chapter, we have proposed a filter technique for multi-label feature selection called FW-MCDM. FW-MCDM has used modified TOPSIS using the KNN algorithm. To prove its preeminence, it has been compared with TOPSIS over four benchmark multi-label datasets. The dataset contains two types of data including text and images. We have achieved significant improvement in different multi-label learning evaluation parameters such as accuracy, hamming loss, ranking loss, coverage, one error and average precision. FW-MCDM has been tested by selecting the top 10/20/30/40 ranked features. However, the proposed method must be compared with other filter techniques. In future, we wanted to explore other MCDM techniques.

References

[1] Kashef, Shima, and Hossein Nezamabadi-pour. 2019. "A Label-Specific Multi-Label Feature Selection Algorithm Based on the Pareto Dominance Concept." *Pattern Recognition* 88 (April): 654–67. https://doi.org/10.1016/j.patcog.2018.12.020.

[2] Spolaôr, Newton, Maria Carolina Monard, Grigorios Tsoumakas, and Huei Diana Lee. 2016. "A Systematic Review of Multi-Label Feature Selection and a New Method Based on Label Construction." *Neurocomputing* 180 (March): 3–15. https://doi.org/10.1016/j.neucom.2015.07.118.

[3] Gao, Wanfu, Liang Hu, and Ping Zhang. 2018. "Class-Specific Mutual Information Variation for Feature Selection." *Pattern Recognition* 79 (July): 328–39. https://doi.org/10.1016/j.patcog.2018.02.020.

[4] Lee, J. and D. W. Kim, 2015b. "Fast Multi-Label Feature Selection Based on Information-Theoretic Feature Ranking." *Pattern Recognition* 48 (9): 2761–71. https://doi.org/10.1016/j.patcog.2015.04.009.

[5] Lee, Jaesung, and Dae Won Kim. 2013. "Feature Selection for Multi-Label Classification Using Multivariate Mutual Information." *Pattern Recognition Letters* 34 (3): 349–57. https://doi.org/10.1016/j.patrec.2012.10.005.

[6] Huang, Jun, Feng Qin, Xiao Zheng, Zekai Cheng, Zhixiang Yuan, Weigang Zhang, and Qingming Huang. 2019. "Improving Multi-Label Classification with Missing Labels by Learning Label-Specific Features." *Information Sciences* 492 (August): 124–46. https://doi.org/10.1016/j.ins.2019.04.021.

[7] He, Zhi Fen, Ming Yang, Yang Gao, Hui Dong Liu, and Yilong Yin. 2019. "Joint Multi-Label Classification and Label Correlations with Missing Labels and Feature Selection." *Knowledge-Based Systems* 163 (January): 145–58. https://doi.org/10.1016/j.knosys.2018.08.018.

[8] Huang, Rui, Weidong Jiang, and Guangling Sun. 2018. "Manifold-Based Constraint Laplacian Score for Multi-Label Feature Selection." *Pattern Recognition Letters* 112 (September): 346–52. https://doi.org/10.1016/j.patrec.2018.08.021.

[9] Lee, J. and D. W. Kim2015a. "Memetic Feature Selection Algorithm for Multi-Label Classification." *Information Sciences* 293 (February): 80–96. https://doi.org/10.1016/j.ins.2014.09.020.

[10] Lim, Hyunki, and Dae Won Kim. 2020. "MFC: Initialization Method for Multi-Label Feature Selection Based on Conditional Mutual Information." *Neurocomputing* 382 (March): 40–51. https://doi.org/10.1016/j.neucom.2019.11.071.

[11] Hashemi, Amin, Mohammad Bagher Dowlatshahi, and Hossein Nezamabadi-pour. 2020. "MFS-MCDM: Multi-Label Feature Selection Using Multi-Criteria Decision Making." *Knowledge-Based Systems* 206 (October). https://doi.org/10.1016/j.knosys.2020.106365.

Chapter 5

Lung Cancer and Pneumonia Detection Using Image Processing and Machine Learning

Preeti Yadav*

Department of Computer and Science, Vipra College Raipur, Raipur, Chhattisgarh, India

Abstract

In medical applications, image processing techniques are a widely used treatment for the diagnosis of Lung cancer tumors and pneumonia predictions. Detection of such tumors and pneumonia at the initial stage is necessary. Many of the research developed methods to test CT (Computed Tomography) scan images, which mostly take four steps: image enhancement, image segmentation, feature extraction of images, and classification of images. Severe pneumonic conditions in the lungs cause death and the reason for lung cancer reside unclearly, prevention is not possible, so identification at an early stage is the way to cure lung cancer and pneumonia. Hence, a lung cancer detection system using image processing and machine learning is used to identify the presence of lung pneumonia in CT- images and X-ray Images.

Keywords: image enhancement, segmentation, feature extraction, classification, filter, preprocessing, threshold

---

* Corresponding Author's Email: preetiyadav2104@gmail.com.

In: Applications of Artificial Intelligence in the Healthcare Sector
Editors: Jyoti Prakash Patra and Yogesh Kumar Rathore
ISBN: 979-8-88697-502-4

5.1. Introduction

Lung cancer is a disorder in which lung cells change into destructive anomalous cells called cancer cells. Then these cancer cells combined and form a cluster known as tumors. Once cancer starts in the human body, it destroys the other healthy cells and subsequently affects the blood cells responsible for taking out the useless substance from the human body. The most common Types of Lung Cancers are "Small Cell Lung Cancer" and "Non-Small Cell Lung cancer" Small Cell Lung Cancer occurs due to smoking and spreads rapidly in the human body, whereas non-small cell cancer grows slowly and occurs due to harmful cells in the human body.

Cancer cells can be passed through the lungs in blood or lymph fluid and surround lung tissue.

Lung cancer symptoms might include:

- Breathing Problem
- Dry or cold Cough
- Heavy pain in the Chest area.
- Issues facing taking a long breath.
- Wheezing.
- Projection blood.
- Feeling dull and tired trough out the day.
- Suddenly loss of weight.

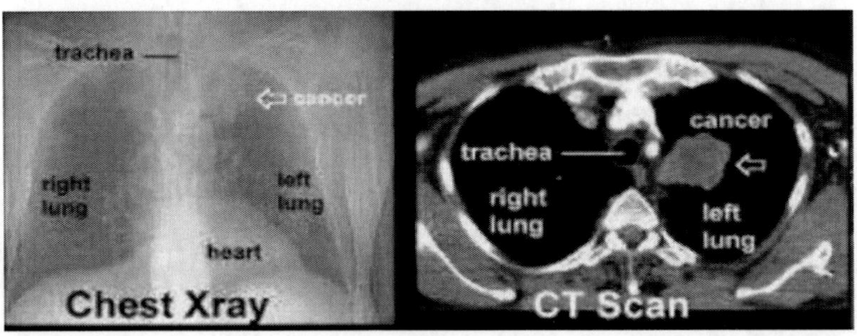

Figure 5.1. Chest x-ray and CT scan of lung.

CT scan is the most sensitive and specific detection method that produces a cross-sectional image of a specific area, with the help of a CT scan, small nodules of lung cancer can be detected. CT scanning is fast, painless, noninvasive, and accurate in lung cancer detection (See Figure 5.1). When we detect Lung cancer using image processing techniques, then we can apply this in various stages like image enhancement, image segmentation, image feature extraction, and classification (See Figure 5.2)

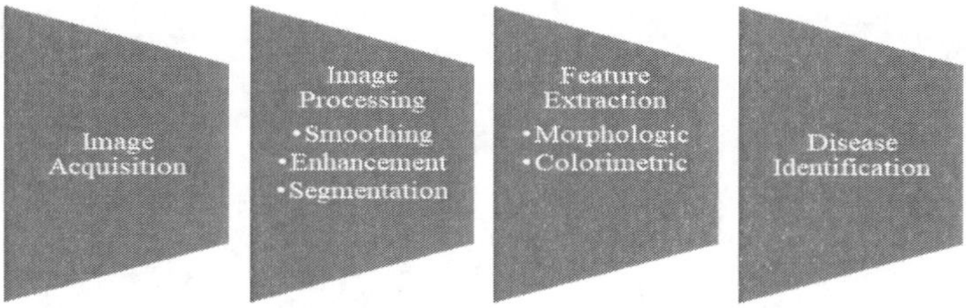

Figure 5.2. Image processing steps.

Deep learning algorithms and techniques are also used for lung cancer screening, training models with large, labeled data sets, and neural network architectures that learn features directly from the data without the need for manual feature extraction. A deep neural network combines a couple of layers like the convolutional neural network layer, Relu activation function, pooling layer, and fully connected layer in deep. All these layers work as a hidden layer of the traditional neural network model. So, including an input layer, numerous hidden layers, and an output layer. The layers are connected by nodes, and neurons and each hidden layer uses the previous layer output as its input (See Figure 5.3).

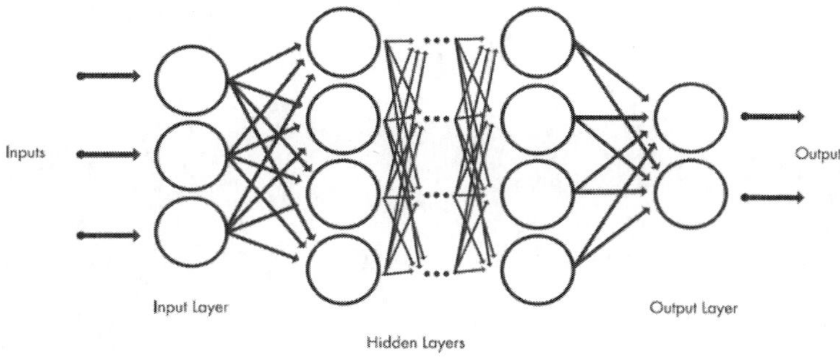

Figure 5.3. CNN model [1].

Convolutional Neural Network (CNN) is the most famous type of deep neural network model, and it is best suited for two-dimensional data processing, like images. CNN works by image feature extraction directly from images. CNNs use 10 or 100 image hidden layers to detect different features of an image. The Number of hidden layers may be increased to extract the more complex features from the input image [1] (See Figure 5.4).

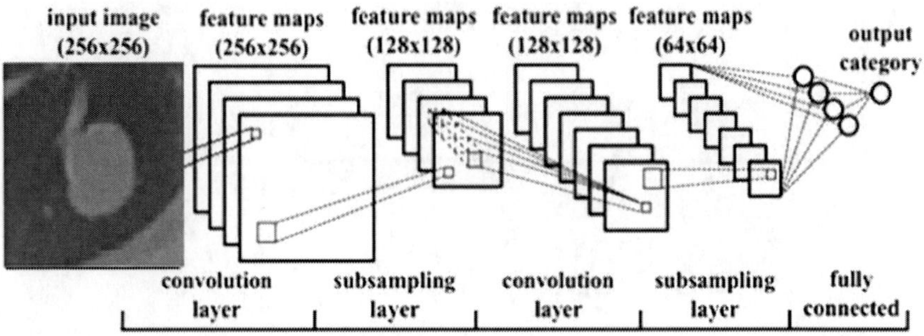

Figure 5.4. Lung cancer detection using CNN [1].

Machine learning algorithms are also widely used for the detection of Lung Cancer. In Machine learning, relevant features of images are manually extracted from images. These features are then used for model creation that categorizes the objects in the image, and various machine learning models like computer-aided diagnosis (CAD) and Artificial Neural Networks (ANN), etc. are used for the detection of Lung cancer. Pneumonia is a disease in the lungs that is caused by bacteria that infect the lung tissue. Pneumonia is a cause of death in many patients. So it is required to detect pneumonia in the early stages. Chest radiography is taken into consideration as the fine diagnostic check for pneumonia in symptomatic patients. Findings on chest radiography encompass lobar consolidation, interstitial infiltrates, and cavitation Danowitz and Mandell (2000), Toltzis et al., (1999), Mandell et al., (2003).

5.1.1. Pneumonia Diagnosis

The following tests are performed on a patient to detect pneumonia, they will give, including:

- Blood tests- for checking the signs of a bacterial infection
- A chest X-ray- for finding the lungs infection percentage in the body
- Pulse oximetry- for measuring the oxygen level in blood
- A sputum test -for finding the fluid in the lungs for the reason of an infection.

5.1.2. Pneumonia Complications

- Bacteremia => in this in your blood bacteria spread. This can be a reason for organ failure and septic shock
- Trouble breathing => in this a person is not able to breathe and he has to take the help of a breathing machine to heal the lungs
- Fluid buildup among the layers of tissue that line your lungs and chest cavity. This fluid also can come to be infected. Lung abscess,
- While a pocket of pus bureaucracy inner or round your lung.

5.1.3. Types of Pneumonia

- Bacterial pneumonia.
- Viral pneumonia.
- Mycoplasma pneumonia.
- Fungal pneumonia.

5.2. Literature Survey

5.2.1. Image Processing-Based Approach

The literature review on respiratory organ unwellness diagnosing (LDD) goes to check the assorted article involving carcinoma unwellness that applies image process techniques on X-radiation (CT) and X-ray images. D. Pan et al., [2], have developed the adaptive threshold algorithm, to diagnose lung disease by CAD system, various image processing methods like image enhancement, and segmentation are performed on CT lung images. Manikandan T et al., [3] proposed that the CAD Comp. Assisted Diagnosis can detect lung cancer at the early stage by the use of CT images, he proposed four steps to detect nodules in the lung cancer patient. In the first step, noise is removed by using different filters, the second step is the segmentation of images, the third step is feature extraction and in the fourth step extracted features from the lungs are classified.

Thresholding-based segmentation has been proposed by T. Agrawal et al., [4], to separate the cancer portion from the input image. Furthermore, Grey Level Correlation Matrix (GLCM) is used to calculate the texture features of the image. The proposed methodology can classify cancer more accurately than the traditional approaches because it uses grey-level features along with statistical and geometric features for the classification. Rupak Bhakta [5] proposed a technique, a quick and strong Fuzzy c-means clustering set of rules is used for the segmentation of lung tumors from the CT because of its accuracy thinking about robustness in opposition to noise and much less computational complexity. First, the lung CT slices have segmented the usage of the FRFCM set of rules, morphological reconstruction is used for image enhancement of FRFCM. The technique used right here is segmentation, feature extractions, and type strategy via way of means of the usage of ground and shape primarily based on filtering. The tumor part is highlighted after the segmentation of the image. The overall performance of the technique is evaluated in phrases of the 3 parameters i.e., sensitivity (SE), specificity (SP), and accuracy.

Sensitivity (SE) determines the ability to appropriately detected positive cases given in eq. (1)

$$SE = TP/(TP + FN) \tag{1}$$

Specificity measures (SP) determine the ability to appropriately detected negative cases given in eq. (2)

$$SP = TN/(FP + TN) \tag{2}$$

Accuracy determines the proportion of correctly classified events given in (3)

$$\text{Accuracy} = (TP + TN)/(TP + FP + TN + FN) \tag{3}$$

where TP, TN, FP, and FN denote true positive, true negative, false positive, and false negative respectively.

Xinyan Li S. F. et al., [6], use kernel graphs cut algorithm and mathematical solution on lung CT-image to detect lung cancer. Hanan M. et al., [7] proposed a method where preprocessing, segmentation, feature extraction, and classification of Lung CT images are performed. To analyze the performance of the model, they used three different classifiers, Multi-layer Feed-forward Neural Network (MF_NN), Radial Basis Function Neural Network (RB-NN), and Support Vector Machine (SVM), and their performance is compared to assess the performance of the proposed system, three quantitative parameters were used to compare the classifier performance: the classification accuracy rate (CAR), the sensitivity (S) and the Specificity (SP). This method has classification accuracy rates (CAR) = 99.6%,), and Specificity (SF) = 100%.

Silva, Carvalho, et al., [8], proposed a machine on how the lung nodule diagnosing the usage of Gini Coefficient and skeletonization methods M. Antonelli B. et al., [9], advanced a technique computerized identity pulmonary aerenchyma integrates the thresholding, morphological operation, border thinning, aspect recognition, aspect reconstructing and additionally filling the region. The motive of this technique is to use the automated identification of the form of the lung with the identical it additionally recovers the unfilled place of the lung and makes the entered dataset prepared for the CAD machine.

K. Kanazawa et al., [10]. The underlying concept of growing a CAD machine isn't always to delegate the analysis to a gadget, however as a substitute that a gadget set of rules acts as a guide to the radiologist and factors out places of suspicious objects so that the general sensitivity is raised. Suren Makaju et al., [11], use a Median filter and Gaussian filter for preprocessing of Computed Tomography (CT) images, and a watershed segmentation algorithm is used to identify cancer nodules and SVM classification is also used in this paper to classify cancer. In the watershed segmentation, the processed image is segmented and some features like the Centroid of the cancer part, and the area of cancer are calculated as input features, and some other features are extracted by the Mean Intensity of the pixel. Finally, for classification purposes, many machine learning classifiers including Support Vector Machines trained from the extracted features to check the accuracy of testing data.

The basic support vector machine (SVM) classifier is a supervised machine learning technique that can be trained using features and can detect the labels of the testing data.

The function is defined in equations (4) and (5), where xi is training inputs, wT is the m-dimensional vector, and b is the bias term.

Here, i = 1…. M.

$$D(x) = wTxi + b \geq 1 \text{ for } yi = 1 \quad (4)$$

$$D(x) = wTxi + b \leq -1 \text{ for } yi = -1 \quad (5)$$

Table 5.1. Comparison of various techniques

Author	Methods	Features	Limitations/challenges	Performance measure
Manikandan T. [3]	CAD	Increased accuracy	various improvement is required to be done in the Sensitivity, Specificity existing diagnosis system	sensitivity = 0.90
T. Aggrawal et al., [4]	Thresholding and greyscale characteristics	Reduces complexity of data Simplifies the process of recognition and classification	a) The resources and processing time required to compute a new data collection (b)A trained learning machine is needed to advance the classification of malignant nodules, as stated in point.	Accuracy-84%, Sensitivity-97.14%, specificities-53.33%
Govindaraju, S. et al., [12]	segmentation k-mean algorithm	Due to the lack of training time, this is quicker. Implementing it is simple.	a) A large dataset cannot be compatible with it. b) With noisy data, it performs worse. c) By creating improved categorization techniques like Support Vector Machine, the accuracy can be increased.	Accuracy- 90.7%,
Amer, H. M. et al., [13]	Support Vector Machine (SVM)	a) Extremely appropriate with a smaller sample size. b) Sound functionality for the high-dimensional data.	a) It required the image intensity value. b) This is comparatively slow In meeting the expectation for the larger dataset.	accuracy- 96.6%, sensitivity-100% Specificities- 94.2%.
Hanan M. et al., [7]	Segmentation, feature extraction, classification	A high degree of sensitivity has been attained, and the number of false positives per image is reasonable.	There is room for improvement in identifying benign and malignant tumors.	CAR-99.06%, S-100%SP-99.2%.
Suren Makaju [11]	watershed segmentation for detection and SVM for classification of a nodule as Malignant	Improves the accuracy of cancer nodule detection over the best current models. • Classify detected lung cancer as malignant or benign. • Eliminates salt-and-pep noise and speckle noise that can lead to false gun detection	The accuracy has improved, but it is still not at the highest level. H. Close to 100% • Classify cancer only as malignant or benign, not in various stages such as stages I, II, III, and IV.	The accuracy has improved, but it is still not at the highest level. H. Close to 100% • Classify cancer only as malignant or benign, not in various stages such as stages I, II, III, and IV.

D. Lin et al., [14] take advantage of the region of interest (ROI) attributes such as size, circularity, and mean brightness. The parameters that were extracted include area, thickness, circularity, intensity, variance, localization, and separation from the lung wall. A comparison of various techniques is shown in Table 5.1.

5.2.2. Machine Learning and Deep Learning-Based Approach

A machine learning-based method, which was a combination of neural network and principle component analysis was proposed by M. Melesh et al., [15] to detect lung cancer from CT scanned images. The researchers compare the performance of the 11 training algorithms: trained, trained, traingdx, trainrp, traincgf, traincgp, traincgb, trainscg, trainbfg, trainoss, and trainlm.

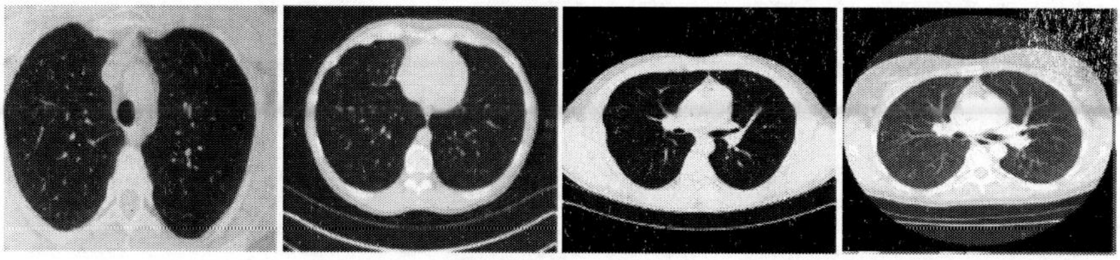

Figure 5.5. Normal lung CT images.

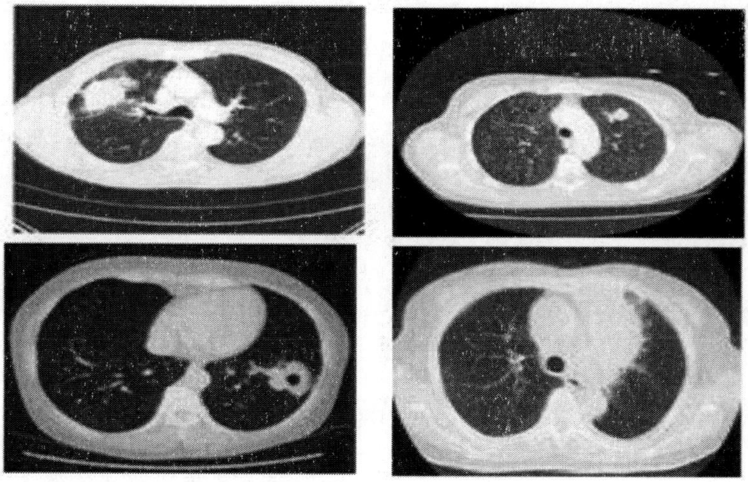

Figure 5.6. Abnormal lung CT images.

The trainlm training algorithm discovers the best detection accuracy of 100% with the least amount of features, with 100% specificity and 100% sensitivity. For testing the effectiveness of the MLNNs detection classifier trained by 11 training algorithms using ICA, the researcher utilizes a dataset of 460 CT images (See Figures 5.5 and 5.6).

3D Convolutional Neural Network Techniques are used by Moradi et al., [16] to separate lung cancer nodules from non-nodules. Nodules can be found in a range of sizes, thus they are categorized into four classes based on their size [17]. There are four classifiers employed, and all four classifiers were integrated to yield better results and employed the ReLU activation function. This method utilizes logistic regression and the LUNA16 dataset. A comparison of various machine-learning models is shown in Table 5.2.

Table 5.2. Comparison of various methods

Author	Methods	Features	Limitations	Performance Measure
Kollabhanu Prakash [18]	CNN	a) Fully automatic, manual intervention is not required. Good classifier at feature detection b) High accuracy in image processing classification	a) CNN is always closed Rotation and scaling. b) Easy to overfit due to the complexity of the model structure	Accuracy 95%
Gray, Givens, Keller, J. M., M. R. et al., [19]	K-Nearest Neighbor (KNN)	a) This is faster due to no training time. b) KNN is easy to implement.	a) It is not compatible For large datasets. b) KNN is less functional with noisy data	Detection rate 97%
Jin, X. et al., [16]	Convolution Neural Networks (CNN)	High accuracy in image processing classification reduce the overall cost of the detection and training stage.	the accuracy is unsatisfactory	accuracy-84.6%, sensitivity-82.5% Specificities-86.7%.

5.2.3. Pneumonia Detection Using X-Ray Image

5.2.3.1. Processing Using CNN

The most frequent way to detect pneumonia is using chest X-rays, but only a medical professional can assess the results. To help medical professionals diagnose and maybe treat diseases like pneumonia, convolutional neural networks are designed to tackle the challenging task of disease detection. MRI, CT, and chest x-ray images can all be used to detect pneumonia. Chest x-rays are one of the most economical methods for diagnosing pneumonia but a qualified radiologist is required for diagnosis utilizing a chest x-ray. The detection of pneumonia also uses deep learning (DL) models. To diagnose pneumonia, deep learning (DL) models use advanced feature extraction and classification techniques [1, 20, 21]. Convolutional Neural Network (CNN) [22] also uses methods for object identification and picture classification to diagnose pneumonia. CNN employs unique filters [23].

5.3. Methodology

The methodology used for lung cancer detection uses image processing technology (See Figure 5.7):

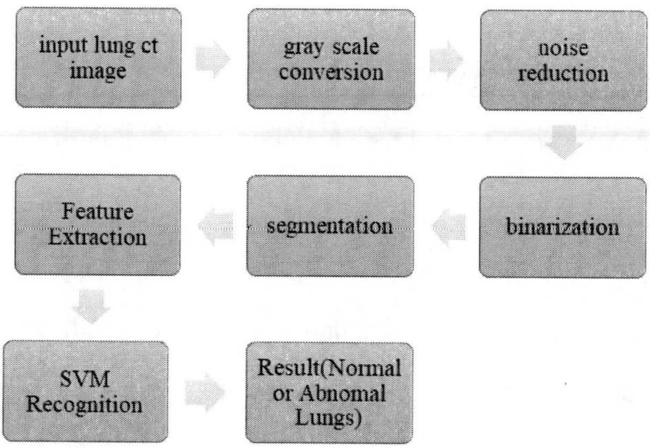

Figure 5.7. Image processing approach.

1. Convert the input image from a color image to a grey scale image.
2. Noise reduction is performed on a grayscale image
3. Perform image segmentation on the grayscale image.
4. Features extraction is performed on an image and features are extracted from its contents like color, texture, shape, position dominant regions of image items and regions, etc.
5. Classifications were performed on the segmented image. SVM (Support Vector Machine) is mostly used for classification.
6. The final result is produced which shows normal and abnormal lungs.

5.3.1. RGB to Grayscale

The conversion of an RGB image to a grayscale image can be done several ways, including the average approach and the weighted method.

Grayscale = (R + G + B) / 3.

5.3.2. Average Method

The average value of R, G, and B is determined as the grayscale value via the Average technique. Grayscale equals (R, G, and B) / 3.

Practically speaking, this formula produces an error because the total of R, G, and B exceeds 255. Calculating R, G, and B separately will help you avoid the exception.

Grayscale = R/3 + G/3 + B/3.

5.3.3. The Weighted Method

According to their wavelengths, red, green, and blue are weighted using this procedure.

=> formula.

The Grayscale is equal to 0.299R + 0.587G + 0.114B.

Figure 5.8. Region-based segmentation.

5.3.4. Image Segmentation

The process of segmenting a digital image into many parts and removing the important area is also known as the zone of interest (ROI).

The region-based segmentation method is shown in Figure 5.8.

*Example = 5 * 5 Image*

5.3.5. Feature Extraction

When there is a large data set and without losing the important data we want to reduce the number of resources then the method of extracting the features is helpful. It reduces the quantity of redundant data from the data set.

Features of the image are extracted from its contents like color, texture, shape, position dominant regions of image items and regions, etc.

5.3.6. SVM (Support Vector Machine) for Classification

SVM is a supervised classification algorithm. In SVM a line is drawn for separating the two categories.

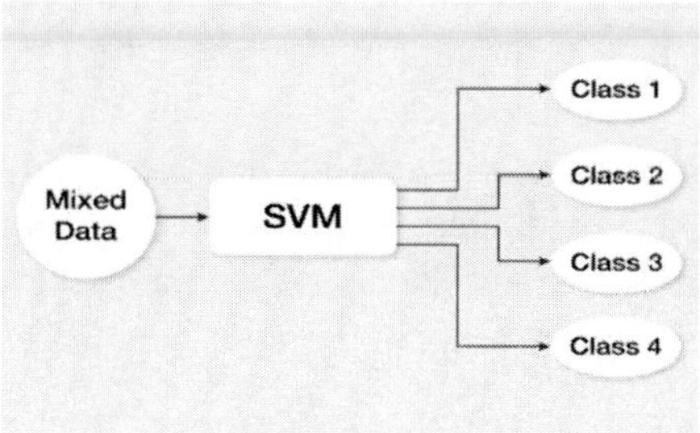

Figure 5.9. Supervised classification algorithm.

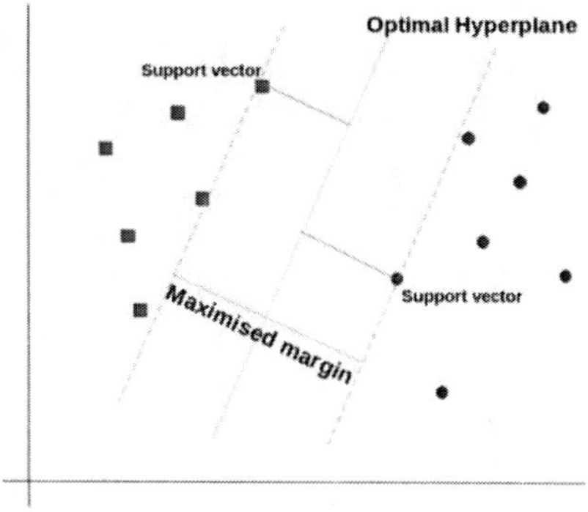

Figure 5.10. Optimal hyperplane.

In the SVM formula, the points highest to the road from each of the categories are determined. These points are known as support vectors. Next, the space between the line and also the support vectors is calculated and it's called the margin. The main goal is to maximize the margin. The best hyperplane for that is the margin ix maximum (See Figures 5.9 and 5.10).

Conclusion

Lung cancer and pneumonia are one of the most dangerous diseases for humans which result in the death of various persons of all age groups various methods are developed by many researchers to detect cancer and pneumonia. Machine learning techniques like KNN, CNN, SVM, etc. are used which give more than 95% accuracy and greater than 85% sensitivity in the input images. Deep learning models became more popular these days because of their capability of classification with high accuracy but have some limitations in terms of the need for a higher-end system to train the data and the need for a high amount of data for training. We suggest the use of pre-trained deep learning models to extract the features from the input image because these models need not train again, it saves time and can extract up to 1000 features from an image. Thereafter, these features cloud be minimized using some feature selection methods and finally, machine learning classifiers may be applied for the task of classification.

References

[1] Lan, K., Dan-tong Wang, Simon Fong, Lian-sheng Liu, Kelvin K. L. Wong & Nilanjan Dey. A survey of data mining and deep learning in bioinformatics. *J. Med. Syst* 42(8) (2018) 139. doi: https://doi.org/10.1007/s10916-018-1003-9.

[2] Chen, S. Feng, and D. Pan. An improved approach of lungs image segmentations based on watershed algorithms, *7th International Conference on Internet Multimedia Computing & Service - ICIMCS '15*. 2015. Zhangjiajie, Hunan, China: ACM New York, NY, USA ©2015.

[3] Manikandan, T. Challenges in the lungs cancers detections using computer aided diagnosis system – a key for survival of patients, *Arch Gen Intern Med* 2017 Vol-1, Issue-2.

[4] Aggarwal, T., Furqan, A., & Kalra, K. Features extractions and LDA based classifications of lungsnodules in chest CT scan image, *2015 International*

Conference on Advances in Computing, Communications And Informatics (ICACCI). https://doi.org/10.1109/ICACCI.2015.7275773.

[5] Bhakta, R. Lung Tumor Segmentation and Staging from CT Images Using Fast and Robust Fuzzy C-Means Clustering. I.J. Image, Graphics and Signal Processing, 2020, 1, 38-45 Published Online February 2020 in MECS (http://www. mecs-press.org/) doi: https://doi.org/10.5815/ijigsp.2020.01.05 Copyright © 2020 MECS I.J. Image, *Graphics and Signal Processing*, 2020, 1, 38-45 Published: 08 February 2020.

[6] Xinyan Li, S. F., Daru Pan. Enhanced lungs segmentations in chests CT images based on kernel graphs cut, *International Conference on Internet Multimedia Computing and Service*. 2016. Xi'an, China:ACM New York, NY, USA ©2016.

[7] Amer, H. M., Fatma E. Z. Abou-Chadi, Sherif S. Kishk, Marwa I. Obayya. A Computer Aided Early Detection model of Pulmonary Nodules in CT Scan Image, *7th International Conference on Software and Information Engineering - ICSIE '18*. 2018, ACM: Cairo, Egypt. p. 81-86.

[8] Silva, A. C., P. C. P. Carvalho, and M. Gattass. Diagnosis of lungs nodules using Gini coefficients and skeletonization in computerized tomography image, *Proceedings of the 2004 ACM symposium on Applied computing - SAC '04*. 2004:Nicosia, Cyprus. https://doi.org/10.1145/967900.967954.

[9] Antonelli, M., B. Lazzerini, and F. Marcelloni, Segmentations and reconstructions of the lungs Vikul J. *Pawar International Journal of Advanced Trends in Computer Science and Engineering*, 9(4), July - August 2020, 5956-5963 5963 volume in CT image, *Proceeding of the 2005 ACM symposium on Applied computing - SAC* '05. 2005.

[10] Kanazawa, K., Y. Kawata, N. Niki, H. Satoh, H. Ohmatsu, R. Kakinuma, M. Kaneko, N. Moriyama and K. Eguchi, "Computer-aideddiagnosis for pulmonary nodules based on helicalCT images," *Compute. Med. Image Graph*, vol. 22, no. 2(1998), pp. 157-167.

[11] Makajua, S., P. W. C. Prasad, Abeer Alsadoon, A. K. Singh, A. Elchouemic India Lung Cancer Detection using CT Scan Images 6th *International Conference on Smart Computing and Communications, ICSCC 2017*, 7-8 December 2017, Kurukshetra.

[12] Sangamithraa, P., & Govindaraju, S. Lungs tumour detection and classifications using K-Mean clustering, *International Conference on Wireless Communication, Signal Processings And Networking (Wispnet)*, 2016.

[13] Amer, H. M., A. Jing Jia, B. Jiwei Liu, C. Yu Gu. A Computer Aided Early Detection model of Pulmonary Nodules in CT Scan Image, *7th International Conference on Software and Information Engineering - ICSIE '18*. 2018, ACM: Cairo, Egypt. p. 81-86.

[14] Lin, D. and C. Yan, "Lung nodules identification rules extraction with neural fuzzy network," *IEEE, Neural Information Processing*, vol. 4, (2002).

[15] Abdelwadood, M. Mesleh "Lung Cancer Detection Using Multi-Layer Neural Networks with Independent Component Analysis: A Comparative Study of Training Algorithms" in *Jordan Journal of Biological Sciences JJBS* Volume 10, Number 4, December 2017 ISSN 1995-6673 Pages 239-249.

[16] Jin, Z. Y., & Jin. Pulmonary Nodules Detections Based on CT Image Using Convolutional Neural Networks, *9th International Symposium on Computational Intelligence And Design*, 2016.

[17] Moradi, P. and Jamzad M. 2019 Detecting Lung Cancer Lesions in CT Images using 3D Convolutional Neural Networks *4th Int. Conf. on Pattern Recognition and Image Analysis* (IPRIA) pp. 114-118.

[18] Prakash, K., Lakshmi Kalyani, Naga Pawan, "Analysis of Mammography for Identifying Cancer Cells Using Convolution Neural network," *IJATCSE* March – April 2020. https://doi.org/10.30534/ijatcse/2020/44922020.

[19] Gray, G., Keller, J. M., M. R. A fuzzy K-NN algorithm, *Transaction IEEE on System, Man, and Cybernetics,* 1985. SMC-15(4): p. 580-585.

[20] Wang, Y., Yating Chen, Ningning Yang, Longfei Zheng, Nilanjan Dey, Amira S. Ashour, Venkatesan Rajinikanth, Joao Manuel R. S. Tavares, Shi Fuqian. Classification of micehepaticgranuloma microscopic images based on a deep convolutional neural network. *Appl. Soft. Comput* 74 (2019) 40-50. doi: https://doi.org/10.1016/j.asoc.2018.10.006.

[21] Ali, M. N. Y., Golam Sarowar, Lizur Rahman, Jyotismita Chaki, Nilanjan Dey, João Manuel R.S. Tavares. Adam deep learning with SOM for human sentiment classification. *International Journal of Ambient Computing and Intelligence (IJACI).* 10(3) (2019) 92-116. doi: https://doi.org/10.4018/IJACI.2019070106.

[22] Song, Q. Z., L. Zhao, X. K. Luo, X. C. Dou, Using deep learning for classification of lung nodules on computed tomography images. *J. Healthc Eng* 2017 (2017) Article ID 8314740, 7 pages. doi: https://doi.org/10.1155/2017/8314740.

[23] Nagi, S. M., Muhammad Sharif, Mussarat Yasmin and Steven Lawrence Fernandes. Lung nodule detection using polygon approximation and hybrid features from CT images. *Curr, Med. Imaging. Rev* 14(1) (2018) 108-117. doi: https://doi.org /10.2174/1573405613666170306114320.

Chapter 6

Deep Learning Algorithms in Healthcare

Suman Kumar Swarnkar[1,*], Bharat Bhushan[2,†] and Tien Anh Tran[3,‡]

[1]Department of Computer Science and Engineering, Shri Shankaracharya Institute of Professional Management and Technology Raipur (C.G.), India
[2]Department of Computer Science and Engineering, Sharda University, Knowledge Park III, Greater Noida, India
[3]Department of Marine Engineering, Vietnam Maritime University Haiphong, Haiphong, Vietnam

Abstract

Artificial neural networks are used in deep learning to identify patterns and make choices based on what they have discovered. Deep learning is a type of machine learning that tries to mimic the way the human brain works by using artificial neural networks. It uses deep learning techniques like regression, classification, and clustering to process large sets of data and identifies relationships between variables. It has become very popular because it is so good at learning from large amounts of data and finding patterns. It has been discovered that deep learning approaches can be used to analyze large amounts of data well. Virtual assistants like Siri and Google now use deep learning to help predict what you will want to know before you even think of it. The purpose of this work is to provide an overview of a number of commonly used deep learning methods as well as their design and implementation in the actual world. This paper also talks about some of the problems with deep learning, like data management, hidden layers, optimization, weights,

* Corresponding Author's Email: sumanswarnkar17@gmail.com.
† Corresponding Author's Email: bharat.bhushan@sharda.ac.in.
‡ Corresponding Author's Email: anhtt.mtb@vimaru.edu.vn.

In: Applications of Artificial Intelligence in the Healthcare Sector
Editors: Jyoti Prakash Patra and Yogesh Kumar Rathore
ISBN: 979-8-88697-502-4

evolution, etc. The advantages and disadvantages of these methods and how they can be used in healthcare, as well as the future of this field, are discussed. The present work gives a literature review of the most common methods to make them easier to use and encourage more innovation in how they can be used. This evaluation will benefit the next specialists in the area of deep learning, where they will learn a lot about the pros, cons, uses, and how different deep learning algorithms work. We also give detailed information on its challenges and application. By including a lot of deep learning challenges in this work, we hope to make more people aware of them and how to deal with them. This could also make researchers more likely to try to find answers to these problems.

Keywords: deep learning, deep Boltzmann machine, deep belief networks, CNN, SVM, KNN, health care

6.1. Introduction

A machine learning technique is a deep learning method that instructs devices and computers on how to think logically. It draws inspiration from the design of the human brain. In contrast to previous machine learning methods, deep learning was first introduced as an artificial neural network (ANN) method, and it has since become much more efficient [1]. Deep learning algorithms continually analyze data in accordance with a predetermined logical framework in an effort to reach conclusions that resemble those of humans. Deep learning enables robots to modify the text, audio, and picture data much as people do in order to carry out human-like activities. Deep learning does this via multi-layered neural network architectures of algorithms. As the name implies, deep learning entails delving deeply into many network levels, including a hidden layer. More sophisticated information is gleaned as one digs deeper. Iterative learning techniques, which deep learning depends on, expose computers to enormous datasets. It aids computers in their ability to recognize characteristics and adapt to changes. After many exposures, machines are able to recognize distinctions across datasets, comprehend the reasoning, and draw trustworthy conclusions [2]. In a review of deep learning was offered. The following details are given in [3]: Multiple processing layers make up computational models. Deep learning lets them learn how to represent data in different ways with different levels of abstraction. These strategies have advanced the state of the art in a number of fields, including identification of visible objects, voice identification, genomics, and drug development, among many others. In order to specify how internal machine parameters must be changed by the machine, back propagation is used in deep learning to locate a complicated structure in a big dataset. These parameters are used to compute the representation inside each layer depending on the previous layer's representation. While CNNs are utilized for the processing of pictures, voice, audio, and video, RNNs are mostly employed for data in a certain order, like audio and text. Many studies in recent years have shown the possibilities of deep learning in a variety of fields, such as medical services and biomedical, including computational biology, biomedical engineering, pervasive sensing, healthcare analytics, public health, motor imagery classification, for improving sensor less FOC efficiency [4], and a novel method created for a self-tuning controller equipped with an FPGA [4]. The purpose of this study is to give a survey of the literature on some widely used deep learning techniques. Our focus is on their strengths, weaknesses, as well as applications, which are things that many scholars in this subject may learn from. Additionally, critical evaluations of several deep learning algorithms are offered, with an emphasis on their benefits, drawbacks, and respective uses. Deep learning methods are also discussed as being used in the medical field. The significance of this study is a systematic analysis of multiple well-known supervised and unsupervised methods, including attention in natural language processing. Several deep learning issues are discussed in this review. The benefits, drawbacks, and applications of these algorithms are also discussed in this literature review, along with whether or not they are supervised or non-supervised. It also addresses how deep learning techniques are used in medicine. As an example, this study provides information on how the COVID-19 epidemic may be combated using deep learning techniques. This report also includes recommendations for further research. This review, which offers comprehensive information on each method, might be useful to researchers who are enthusiastic about using deep learning techniques in the medical field. Additionally, novices and fresh researchers in the area of deep learning may use this research as a preliminary step for a thorough understanding of each learning algorithm, gaining the information they need to solve deep learning-related issues and create new deep learning algorithms.

6.2. Literature Survey

Bioinformatics, medical imaging, ubiquitous sensing, medical informatics, and public health use deep learning. COVID-19 prediction, classification, and detection algorithms are reviewed using deep learning. Deep learning can handle EMG, EEG, EOG, and ECG data successfully (ECG). RNNs and one-dimensional CNNs are often employed [5]. The author suggested utilizing sonar to find targets [6]. Two-layer back propagation networks separated sonar reflections off rocks and metal cylinders in Chesapeake Bay. Two output units complement the 60 inputs. Fourier transform of raw time stream determines input pattern. 12 concealed units worked best (nearly 100 percent training set accuracy). The authors of [6] offered a strategy for healthcare professionals handling a COVID19 crisis that applies techniques of inquiry for the first COVID19 patient suffering with this condition. This work presents a deep learning method for medical image feature extraction. Stacking auto-encoders is used. This approach compresses images for faster retrieval and comparison. Given the capabilities of stacked encoders, the auto-encoder approach in a content-based image retrieval system offers 80% accuracy for COVID-19 digital photographs [7]. Also, cancer diagnostic auto encoder methods exist. Sparse auto encoders are used to recognize micro aneurysms in diabetic retinopathy fundus pictures. Using FMRI, 3D brain reconstruction, and cell clustering, auto-encoder-based learning algorithms may predict Alzheimer's disease progression [8]. Cancer patient multi-omic and clinical data were auto-encoders [9]. They studied these methodologies and established a clear foundation for establishing cancer-study and treatment systems. They explained how to design, administer, and utilize integrated breast cancer data networks. These strategies provide relevant data representations for accurate diagnosis. RBM designs may identify suicide risk in mental health patients and segment multiple sclerosis lesions in multi-channel 3D MRIs utilizing low-dimensional approaches (EHR). Depending on a patient's clinical state, they may also recognize photoplethysmography signals [10]. Classifying hyper spectral medical images that are difficult to categorize using deep learning is the focus of this study. Using an unsupervised generative model known as a bipartite deep Boltzmann machine (DBM) architecture, we were able to do this. A back-propagation topology in a three-layer unsupervised network serves as the implementation's base. Discriminative and non-discriminative image patches are collected in the present dataset and categorized into two groups: Spatial data is used to create spectral-spatial images of categorization labels. Class labelling is used to calculate the accuracy, false-positive prediction rate (FPR), and sensitivity of the fully connected network. An accuracy of 95.5 percent and a sensitivity of 93.5 percent were attained using the suggested cognitive computation approach. The computer-aided identification of malignant areas in HIS (hyperspectral imaging) pictures is significantly improved by the DBM model. In the initial stage of this approach, informative and non-discriminative picture patches are divided. During the second learning phase, the DBM's accuracy and success rate were calculated. CNN's technique was 6.1% less accurate. Unsupervised DBM successfully detected cancerous regions in 3D hyper spectral images [11]. DBNs can detect anomalies, monitor biological parameters, identify obstacles, interpret sign language, diagnose lifestyle disorders, and predict infectious disease outbreaks [12]. Chest X-ray pictures were utilized to identify healthy and COVID-19 patients using deep belief networks [13] with a 90% accuracy rate, the suggested approach effectively locates COVID-19 instances. The appearance of a white, patchy shadow in the lungs often serves as the basis for the diagnosis. It can identify these illnesses from these medical photos by applying a Gaussian filter (to reduce noise). The crucial lung region is then distinguished from the others to separate the medical imaging [14]. Threshold-based segmentation is used to differentiate the lungs that have been impacted by COVID-19 from the normal lungs. Retinal fundus photographs can be used to detect diabetic retinopathy, skin cancer can be classified by dermatologists [15], CHD can be predicted from longitudinal EHRs, COPD can be predicted from longitudinal EHRs, sleep quality can be predicted from daytime activity data, and EEG can be detected using CNN algorithms. Early onset Alzheimer's disease (AD) and MCI are connected (MCI). Early identification of Alzheimer's disease might be improved by using voxel-based hierarchical feature extraction, according to some researchers (VHFE) [16]. An automatic labelling template was used to partition the brain into 90 ROIs (AAL Based on voxel correlations, the first-stage characteristics were established. Brain voxel maps were put into a convolutional neural network (CNN) in order to discover previously unknown characteristics in the brain (CNN). Reliable and encouraging outcomes have been shown by the data [17]. CNN makes extensive use of spatially invariant input, such as pictures whose meanings do not change as they are translated. Physicians may benefit from the use of deep learning algorithms, which may provide alternative opinions and raise issues. CNNs can categorize pictures much like humans. First, they are trained on a large dataset that has nothing to do with their purpose of understanding natural statistics in photos (curves, straight lines, colorations, etc.) [18]. Picture of a doctor Algorithms at the highest levels are retrained to recognize diagnostic conditions. The use of CNNs helped students study. Doctors are able to detect large-arterial occlusions in the brain with the use of image segmentation and object recognition [19] (a few minutes). Mitotic cells [20] and tumor areas [21] may also be detected using CNNs. CNNs can predict survival based on their grasp of tissue biology [22]. LSTM's Clinical measurements in critical care units, predictive medicine based on patient history, and de-identification of patient clinical data are all being explored using RNNs [23]. A speech translation system based on RNNs has been developed. Electronic health records (EHRs) may benefit from the transcription of patient-provider conversations using this method (EHRs). It's important to summarize the topic while labeling each medical component. Clinical voice assistants may benefit from next-generation speech recognition and information extraction models (versions 35 and 36) by recording patient interactions. Human-computer interaction (HCI) has the potential to improve medical care, according to early studies [24]. To enable communication between humans and machines, BCI measures brain activity. In terms of practicality and non-invasiveness, electroencephalography is the best option (EEG). SNR and spatial resolution are both severely constrained. There is a novel method that uses convolutional neural networks, continuous wavelet transform, and blind source separation to estimate independent components (CNN). Modern techniques have a success rate of 94.66 percent. Even though the number of convolutions has minimal impact on CNN accuracy, hyper-parameters like kernel size and kernel stride have an impact on network performance [25]. Explains how reconfigurable hardware may be used to build an open-architecture servo controller [26]. Position, speed, and acceleration are all outputs of the servo system [27]. To enhance servo control and eliminate linear motion system vibration, the authors developed an online self-tuning genetic approach [28]. To build the controller, we used open-source graphical and logical programming software. Using this method, updates and tweaks are simple, decreasing obsolescence. Python provides speed profiling and controller tweaking, as well as the ability to measure parameters and monitor servo system vibration. PID controller for linear movement system has been created to automatically alter the trajectory. The modules may be used by FPGA makers [29]. As a result, open-source solutions outperform their proprietary counterparts. Windows, Linux, and Mac OS X may all use it. System variables and vibrations may be monitored using a Python GUI developed by the authors. Trapezoidal velocity profiles may be computed and serial gains can be set up using this GUI. Simply alter the technique used to calculate the profile's velocity to run tests on various profiles. Translational mechatronics' PID controller can monitor any route within 0.2 percent. Translational mechatronic systems may benefit from vibration monitoring. Maintaining the vehicle in good working order [30]. CMAC-ADALINE and FOC are used in this study to compare the real-time and online estimates of electrical parameters. The CMAC-ADALINE enhances the performance and longevity of the induction motor driver. The speed and resistance of an induction motor rotor were calculated using neural networks, according to the scientists. A novel estimator for neural networks and control theory was provided in the study. The enhanced performance of the IM driver may be attributed to the verification of the speed and rotor resistance estimations.

Table 6.1. Deep learning methods are employed accurately in a variety of areas

S. No.	Reference No.	Algorithm Used	Domain	Accuracy Rate
1	Benyelles, F.Z. et al.	Back propagation	Sonar target recognition	Nearly 100%
2	Ravì, D. et al.	Stacked auto-encoders	Recognition of COVID-19 digital pictures.	80%
3	Block, H.D et al.	DBM	For the detection of malignant areas in hyperspectral medical pictures classification.	95.5%
4	Abdulrahman, S.A. et al.	DBN	Medical pictures from chest X-rays are used to classify people as either normal or having COVID-19 disease.	90%
5	Yue, L. et al.	Convolutional Neural Network	A voxel-based hierarchical feature extraction approach may be used to diagnose Alzheimer's disease.	97%
6	Ortiz-Echeverri, C.J. et al.	Convolutional Neural Network	Based on the sorted blind source separation method for classifying motor imagery images.	94.66%
7	Islam, M.M. et al.	Convolutional Neural Network	to look for COVID	99%
8	Islam, M.M. et al.	Deep Neural Network	to look for COVID	99.7%
9	Islam, M.M. et al.	Support Vector Machine	to look for COVID	99.68%
10	Islam, M.M. et al.	K- Neural Network	to look for COVID	93.41%
11	Reyes, L.M.S. et al.	DBN & CDBN	COVID-19 must be detected in chest X-ray pictures.	99.93%
12	Atinza, R. et al.	Support Vector Machine and neural network	Dementia illnesses may be detected using this method.	90%

A hybrid neural network estimator with two different designs worked as expected. The FOC efficiency of this estimator is improved by changing the weights of the rotor and the speed at which it rotates. There was a low error rate over three-phase intermodulation (IM) while using this method of measuring resistance. An artificial neural network-based self-adjusting PID controller was devised in previous research [30]. Network gains are determined based on the system's transient and stationary response components. The network's maximum desirable overshoots, settling periods, and stationary errors were also inputs, in addition to the error for network training. To collect PID gain response data, an offline training database was built using evolutionary methods. Stable growth may be used by genetic algorithms to gather data throughout a wide variety of operational ranges. For educational purposes, the database was used. The neural network came up with a gain combination after taking into account the mistake and the expected response. The method's effectiveness was tested by varying the speed of a direct-current motor. On average, the system responds to database queries with a 4% error rate. The network's predictions were steady in 86% of dataset combinations tested (1544 connections). There are several advantages and disadvantages to each of the deep learning algorithms that have been discussed in this article (See Table 6.1).

6.3. Healthcare Application Using Deep Learning Method

COVID-19 is being treated using deep learning approaches. Healthcare globally uses deep learning. These programmes analyze photographs, categorize data, and predict when things will normalize. 4.4 million individuals have died from COVID-19. Virus threatens humanity. Deep learning wasn't viable until COVID-19 because it requires a lot of training data and processing resources. Deep learning is incomprehensible. COVID-19 recommends further research on classification, screening, and diagnosis. Machine learning and deep learning were used to predict, identify, and diagnose COVID-19. Convolutional neural networks, deep neural networks, and support vector machines identify infections 98% accurately. Deep learning discovered COVID-19, viral pneumonia, and healthy chest X-rays. COVID-19 may be identified using COVID-DeepNet [31]. Radiologists can quickly analyze images using this approach. Deep belief networks are integrated. The discovered approach may be utilized to diagnose COVID-19 early. Since each photo pick lasts less than three seconds, it can measure therapy efficacy. ConvoNet CNN, Covid-Net CNN, and CoroNet, Auto Encoders delivers accurate diagnosis. WOA-CNN, CRNet, and CNNs CT-scan datasets include COVID-19. Deep learning uses CT to diagnose and predict COVID-19 [31]. 7 cities or provinces provided 5273 CT images. 4106 CT images were used to train the deep learning algorithm. The deep learning system was trained on 1266 patients. 924 COVID-19 patients had longer-term follow-up. 342/1266 people had pneumonia. Deep learning differentiated COVID-19 from viral and other pneumonia. Deep learning can also classify patients by hospital stay. Deep learning can swiftly identify high-risk patients and diagnose COVID-19, helping patients before important phases. It is categorized tissue using SegNet and U-NET. SegNet segments scenes while U-NET segments medical images [31]. SegNet and U-NET were utilized to distinguish sick lung tissue [31]. Both networks may act as multi-class segmentors [31]. Each network was assessed on 18 photographs after training on 72 [31]. SegNet could distinguish healthy versus sick tissues. U-multi-class NET segmentor-based results were better [31]. Neural networks can anticipate future vaccination patterns [31]. Unsupervised learning was used to forecast the active virus's geographic spread in the USA. Machine learning may be used to plan population dose. In certain countries, algorithms predict cases and fatalities. Deep learning's improved prediction accuracy enables data-driven lockdown decisions. A case study in India predicted the shutdown duration without taking outside factors into consideration. A linear regression model projected how long India's lockdowns will be [32]. It is evaluated how deep learning affects COVID-19 and suggested further research. Writers offer deep learning applications in NLP, epidemiology, and biology. [32] contrasted big data and learning issue applications. COVID-19 describes deep learning's limits. Data privacy, sparse labelling, and generalization metrics are restrictions. Deep learning predicts COVID-19 cases and deaths. Multivariate CNN outperformed LSTM in accuracy and consistency. CNN is recommended for long-term forecasting without seasonality and periodic patterns [32]. DL methods help diagnose COVID-19 quickly and precisely. Deep learning was used to diagnose COVID19 patients. People enjoy TL and CNN. AI may be utilized for pharmaceutical development, clinical image analysis, and coronavirus pandemic predictions. In the lack of diagnostic criteria, many persons with suspected COVID-19 pneumonia should undergo a CT scan following a CXR. DNNs start from scratch [32]. Deep learning apps will identify COVID-19 indicators, AI-powered robots will maintain social distance, medical records will be kept on the blockchain, and big data will follow COVID-19's advancement. The outbreak was ended [33]. Using retrospectively obtained CT images from multiple scanners and facilities, the authors created a poorly supervised deep learning architecture for COVID-19 recognition and classification. It's different from CAP and NP (non-pneumonia). It may also detect COVID-19-caused lesions or inflammations and provide triage and therapeutic information. The recommended model visualizes lesions correctly [33]. CXR scans are used to identify COVID-19 pneumonia from healthy lungs (in a normal individual). GM convolutional neural networks were employed (GDCNN). It extracts COVID-19 features and common photographs. The new method is better. The COVID-19 prediction is accurate, precise, sensitive, and specific [33]. Deep learning-based recommender systems may detect COVID-19 if there are numerous patients and minimal radiological knowledge. Four deep CNN architectures were used to diagnose COVID-19 chest X-rays. Mobilenet is great. CNN-based approaches properly diagnose COVID-19. Transfer learning improves detection. Experimentation may improve these models' accuracy. Using chest X-rays, this research demonstrated a deep learning-based clinical decision support system for early COVID-19 diagnosis. Three-stage design. Before adding data, images are preprocessed. Second, educate. Third-stage classification and prediction use a fully-linked network of classifiers. The proposed deep learning system has an AUC of 0.97 for internal validation and 0.95 for external validation. This research shows how AI improves COVID-19 imaging. AI-powered CT and X-rays prove COVID-19's effectiveness. COVID-19 patients aren't imageable. Imaging data, clinical symptoms, and lab test results enhance COVID-19 screening, identification, and diagnosis. AI will use data from multiple sources for diagnosis, analysis, and follow-up. This paper discusses AI-powered modelling tools. Field expertise and AI-driven technologies must start gathering data jointly. Use many data types to make confident judgments. Active learning is studied using multimodal, longitudinal data [33]. AI was used to identify COVID-19 CTs quickly. Over 10,000 CT images from COVID-19, influenza-A/B, CAP and other illnesses were utilized. The deep convolutional neural network-based technique got 97.81% AUC on 3199 scans. In a reading study, our AI system beat five radiologists. COVID-19 was found in 2020. COVID-19 symptoms include fever, respiratory difficulties, dry cough, headaches, runny noses, nasal obstructions, body pains, and throat discomfort.

6.4. Challenges of Deep Learning

This section talks about some of the problems that come with deep learning.

6.4.1 AutoML-Zero

"AutoML" automates ML algorithm design and development [34]. AutoML has already assembled manually-created complicated components into solutions. Instead of manually-built sophisticated components, look for full algorithms. This is a difficulty since it requires searching enormous, sparse regions. Despite this, automating ML has advantages. Without previous knowledge bias, new ML designs may be conceivable [34]. A generic search space reduces human bias, which explains this. AutoML uses evolution to automate generating entire ML algorithms from the outset using basic mathematical processes [34]. Backpropagation training may discover two-layer neural networks, which evolution seeks. By developing after each challenge, neural networks may be exceeded.

6.4.2. Neural Architecture Search

Manually creating neural networks by ML and deep learning experts may be time-consuming and error-prone. NAS is popular. NAS automates neural network build. NAS enables better-planned structures for object detection and photo classification. NAS approaches are categorized by search space, strategy, and performance estimate.

6.4.3. Evolutionary Deep Learning

Deep neural network designs, hyperparameter adjustments, and training are key to their performance in a number of applications and for handling varied difficulties. Architectural searching research may be classified into two categories: reinforcement learning and natural selection. [35] mention evolving deep neural networks. (EAs). They're famous for having no gradient. These algorithms rely on population but can identify multiple search space sites and avoid local optimums [35].

6.4.4. Data Management Challenges

Data collection, exploration, preprocessing, dataset preparation, testing, deployment, and postal distribution are detailed in Reference [36]. Deep learning practitioners can handle these challenges [36].

6.4.5. Quantity of Input and Identification of Noncontributing Attributes

Identifying non-contributing features and managing inputs are challenges [37]. A dataset may have several features. Deep learning models ignore unneeded attributes. Separate the dataset and attribute class. Choosing a valuable attribute is hard.

6.4.6. Activation Functions

It may be hard to determine where to use activation functions [37]. Sigmoid activation function works well for binary classification. If vanishing gradients are present, apply tanh cautiously. Multi-labelled categorization uses softmax activation. If many inputs are zero, use leaky ReLU. ReLU is the most popular activation function because... Cheap computational costs; utilized on hidden network layers.

6.4.7. Kinds of Network

CNN, LSTM, and dense networks are all mentioned [37]. There is a widely used network called LSTM. It's effective and complicated at the same time. Neurons are connected to one another in a dense network layer by layer. It was decided to build a lengthy short-term memory network in order to circumvent issues with long-term memory. The activation function and architecture of the output layer of a generic neural network may vary widely. Weather forecasting [38] makes use of LSTM networks, which are useful when the subsequent layers each have a different architecture. It is possible to compare the results of different CNN layers since each one is fed by the one above it. Image processing and computer vision are among the fields where this technology is being researched.

6.4.8. Epochs

After this point in time, we may consider ourselves lucky. Using the weights at each epoch, a model is built. The weights are altered and evaluated in the following time. During implementation, the RAM must have access to training data. When dealing with huge datasets, keeping the training set in RAM may not be an option. It is thus necessary to partition the data into batches, each of which is implemented and received by the RAM in turn. In a nutshell, the outcome marks the end of an era [39].

Conclusion

Auto encoders, variational auto encoders and limited Boltzmann machines are some of the algorithms covered in this article. Algorithm architectures are described. The advantages, limitations, applications, and supervised/ unsupervised classification of deep learning systems were examined. Deep learning algorithms are contrasted in terms of their usability and precision, and Deep learning algorithms have also been studied in healthcare, specifically their ability to identify between COVID-19 and viral pneumonia using image processing. The lockout may be alleviated or imposed through deep learning. Deep learning methods in medical literature, include COVID-19 algorithms for prediction, classification, and detection. Dementia and cancer may be tackled through deep learning. Future work will use both model-based and model-free deep learning. Using these models, we'll explore their strengths and limitations. Neural architecture search, evolutionary deep learning, etc. In-depth learning alternatives have been presented. Deep learning methodologies, healthcare applications, and deep learning concerns were all examined in this research.

References

[1] McCulloch, W. S.; Pitts, W. A logical calculus of the ideas immanent in nervous activity. *Bull. Math. Biophys.* 1943, 5, 115–133. https://doi.org/10.1007/ BF02478259.

[2] Rosenblatt, F. "The perceptron: a probabilistic model for information storage and organization in the brain." *Psychological review* vol. 65,6 (1958): 386-408. doi:10.1037/h0042519.

[3] Block, H. D. A review of perceptrons: An introduction to computational geometry. *Inf. Control* 1970, 17, 501–522. https://doi.org/10.1016/S0019-9958(70)90409-2.
[4] Werbos, P. J. Beyond Regression: New Tools for Prediction and Analysis in the Behavioral Sciences; Harvard University: Cambridge, MA, USA, 1975. *Inf. Control* 1970, 17, 501–522.
[5] Öngen, Demet Erol. "Cognitive Emotion Regulation in the Prediction of Depression and Submissive Behavior: Gender and Grade Level Differences in Turkish Adolescents." *Procedia - Social and Behavioral Sciences,* vol. 9, 2010, pp. 1516–1523., https://doi.org/10.1016/j.sbspro.2010.12.358.
[6] Fukushima, K. Neocognitron: A hierarchical neural network capable of visual pattern recognition. *Neural Netw.* 1988, 1, 119–130.
[7] Jordan, Michael I. "Serial Order: A Parallel Distributed Processing Approach." *Neural-Network Models of Cognition - Biobehavioral Foundations,* 1997, pp. 471–495., https://doi.org/10.1016/s0166-4115(97)80111-2.
[8] Lecun, Y., Bottou, L., Bengio, Y., Haffner, P. Gradient-based learning applied to document recognition. *Proc. IEEE* 1998, 86, 2278–2324.
[9] Hinton, G. E., Osindero, S., Teh, Y.-W. A Fast Learning Algorithm for Deep Belief Nets. *Neural Comput.* 2006, 18, 1527–1554.
[10] Hinton, G. E. Reducing the Dimensionality of Data with Neural Networks. *Science* 2006, 313, 504–507.
[11] LeCun, Y., Bengio, Y., Hinton, G. Deep learning. *Nature* 2015, 521, 436–444.
[12] Simidjievski, N., Bodnar, C., Tariq, I., Scherer, P., Andres Terre, H., Shams, Z., Shams, Z., Jamnik, M., Liò, P. Variational Autoencoders for Cancer Data Integration: Design Principles and Computational Practice. *Front. Genet.* 2019, 10, 1205.
[13] Miotto, R., Wang, F., Wang, S., Jiang, X., Dudley, J. T. Deep learning for healthcare: Review, opportunities and challenges. *Brief. Bioinform.* 2018, 19, 1236–1246.
[14] Jeyaraj, P. R., Nadar, E. R. S. Deep Boltzmann machine algorithm for accurate medical image analysis for classification of cancerous region. *Cogn. Comput. Syst.* 2019, 1, 85–90.
[15] Shuo Wang, Yunfei Zha, Weimin Li, Qingxia Wu, Xiaohu Li, Meng Niu, Meiyun Wang, Xiaoming Qiu, Hongjun Li, He Yu, Wei Gong, Yan Bai, Li Li, Yongbei Zhu, Liusu Wang and Jie Tian. A fully automatic deep learning system for COVID-19 diagnostic and prognostic analysis. *Eur. Respir. J.* 2020, 56, 2000775.
[16] Chamola, V., V. Hassija, V. Gupta and M. Guizani, "A Comprehensive Review of the COVID-19 Pandemic and the Role of IoT, Drones, AI, Blockchain, and 5G in Managing its Impact," in *IEEE Access,* vol. 8, pp. 90225-90265, 2020, doi: 10.1109/ACCESS.2020.2992341.
[17] Yue, L., Gong, X., Li, J., Ji, H., Li, M., Nandi, A. K. Hierarchical Feature Extraction for Early Alzheimer's Disease Diagnosis. *IEEE Access* 2019, 7, 93752–93760.
[18] Barreira, C. M., Bouslama, M., Haussen, D. C., Grossberg, J. A., Baxter, B., Devlin, T., Frankel, M., Nogueira, R. G. Abstract WP61: Automated Large Artery Occlusion Detection IN Stroke Imaging—ALADIN Study. S*troke* 2018, 49 (Suppl. S1), AWP61.

[19] Cire¸san, D. C., Giusti, A., Gambardella, L. M., Schmidhuber, J. Mitosis Detection in Breast Cancer Histology Images with Deep Neural Networks. In *Medical Image Computing and Computer-Assisted Intervention—MICCAI* 2013; Mori, K., Sakuma, I., Sato, Y., Barillot, C., Navab, N., Eds.; Springer: Berlin/Heidelberg, Germany, 2013; Volume 8150, pp. 411–418.

[20] Liu, Y., Gadepalli, K., Norouzi, M., Dahl, G. E., Kohlberger, T., Boyko, A., Venugopalan, S., Timofeev, A., Nelson, P. Q., Corrado, G. S., Hipp, J. D., Peng, L., & Stumpe, M. C. *Detecting Cancer Metastases on Gigapixel Pathology Images.* arXiv 2017, arXiv:170302442Cs. Available online: http://arxiv.org/abs/1703.02442 (accessed on 29 August 2021).

[21] Beck, A. H., Sangoi, A. R., Leung, S., Marinelli, R. J., Nielsen, T. O., Van De Vijver, M. J., West, R. B., van de Rijn, M., Koller, D. Systematic Analysis of Breast Cancer Morphology Uncovers Stromal Features Associated with Survival. *Sci. Transl. Med.* 2011, 3, 108ra113.

[22] Hong, J., Lee, D., Jeong, E.-R., & Yi, Y. "Towards the Swift Prediction of the Remaining Useful Life of Lithium-Ion Batteries with End-to-End Deep Learning." *Applied Energy,* vol. 278, 2020, p. 115646, https://doi.org/10.1016/j.apenergy.2020.115646.

[23] Chen, Z., Chen, L., Shen, W., Xu, K. Remaining Useful Life Prediction of Lithium-Ion Battery Via a Sequence Decomposition and Deep Learning Integrated Approach. *IEEE Trans. Veh. Technol.* 2021, 414, 245–254.

[24] Islam, M. M., Karray, F., Alhajj, R., Zeng, J. A Review on Deep Learning Techniques for the Diagnosis of Novel Coronavirus (COVID-19). *IEEE Access* 2021, 9, 30551–30572.

[25] Ortiz-Echeverri, C. J., Salazar-Colores, S., Rodríguez-Reséndiz, J., Gómez-Loenzo, R. A. A New Approach for Motor Imagery Classification Based on Sorted Blind Source Separation, Continuous Wavelet Transform, and Convolutional Neural Network. *Sensors* 2019, 19, 4541.

[26] Gutierrez-Villalobos, J. M., Rodriguez-Resendiz, J., Rivas-Araiza, E. A., Martínez-Hernández, M. A. Sensorless FOC Performance Improved with On-Line Speed and Rotor Resistance Estimator Based on an Artificial Neural Network for an Induction Motor Drive. *Sensors* 2015, 15, 15311.

[27] Cruz-Miguel, E. E., García-Martínez, J. R., Rodríguez-Reséndiz, J. Carrillo-Serrano, R. V. A New Methodology for a Retrofitted Self-tuned Controller with Open-Source FPGA. *Sensors* 2020, 20, 6155.

[28] Rodríguez-Abreo, O., Rodríguez-Reséndiz, J., Fuentes-Silva, C., Hernández-Alvarado, R., Falcón MD CP, T. Self-Tuning Neural Network PID with Dynamic Response Control. *IEEE Access* 2021, 9, 65206–65215.

[29] Benyelles, F. Z., Sekkal, A., Settouti, N. Content Based COVID-19 Chest X-ray and CT Images Retrieval framework using Stacked Auto-Encoders. In *Proceedings of the 2nd International Workshop on Human-Centric Smart Environments for Health and Well-being (IHSH),* Boumerdes, Algeria, 9–10 February 2020.

[30] Ravì, D., Wong, C., Deligianni, F., Berthelot, M., Andreu-Perez, J., Lo, B., Yang, G. Z. Deep learning for health informatics. *IEEE J. Biomed. Health Inform.* 2017, 21, 4–21.

[31] Russakovsky, O., Deng, J., Su, H., Krause, J., Satheesh, S., Ma, S., Huang, Z., Karpathy, A., Khosla, A., Bernstein, M., Berg, A. C., & Fei-Fei, L. ImageNet Large Scale Visual Recognition Challenge. *Int. J. Comput. Vis.* 2015, 115, 211–252.

[32] Yosinski, J., Clune, J., Bengio, Y., Lipson, H. *How transferable are features in deep neural networks?* arXiv 2014, arXiv:14111792Cs. Available online: http://arxiv.org/abs/1411.1792 (accessed on 29 August 2021).

[33] Hochreiter, S., Schmidhuber, J. Long Short-Term Memory. *Neural Comput.* 1997, 9, 1735–1780.

[34] Chou, K., Ramsundar, B., Robicquet, A. *A Guide to Deep Learning in Healthcare.* Available online: researchgate.net (accessed on 10 September 2021).

[35] Al-Waisy, A. S., Mohammed, M. A., Al-Fahdawi, S., Maashi, M. S., Garcia-Zapirain, B., Abdulkareem, K. H., Mostafa, S. A., Le, D. N. COVID-DeepNet: Hybrid Multimodal Deep Learning System for Improving COVID-19 Pneumonia Detection in Chest X-ray Images. *Comput. Mater. Contin.* 2021, 67, 2409–2429.

[36] Sánchez-Reyes, Luz-María., Rodríguez-Reséndiz, Juvenal., Avecilla-Ramírez, Gloria Nélida., García-Gomar, María-Luisa., and Robles-Ocampo, Jose-Billerman. Impact of EEG Parameters Detecting Dementia Diseases: A Systematic Review. *IEEE Access* 2021, 9, 78060–78074.

[37] Atinza, R. *Advanced Deep Learning with Keras*; Packt Publishing: Birmingham, UK, 2018. [Google Scholar].

[38] Pumsirirat, A., Yan, L. Credit Card Fraud Detection using Deep Learning based on Auto-Encoder and Restricted Boltzmann Machine. *Int. J. Adv. Comput. Sci. Appl.* 2018, 9, 18–25.

[39] Zrira, N., Khan, H. A., Bouyakhf, E. H. Discriminative Deep Belief Network for Indoor Environment Classification Using Global Visual Features. *Cogn. Comput.* 2018, 10, 437–453.

Chapter 7

Applying Topic Models for Finding N-Gram Entities in Biomedical Literature

G. S. Mahalakshmi[1,*], S. Hemadharsana[1,†], K. Srividhyasaradha[1,‡] and S. Sendhilkumar[2,§]

[1]Department of Computer Science and Engineering, Anna University, Chennai, Tamilnadu, India

[2]Department of Information Science and Technology, Anna University, Chennai, Tamilnadu, India

Abstract

Biomedical research articles have been increasing post-pandemic multi-fold. Search Engines have introduced search tags with Entity and Diseases. To aid this tagging, research articles need to be automatically mined for bio-medical entity names without much expert intervention. This paper discusses the combination of various topic models over auto-encoders to automatically find Topic N-grams (TnG) from scientific research article corpus. The results are very promising when compared with other existing approaches for Entity Labelling.

Keywords: deep learning, correlation, correlated deep topic model, LDA, HDP

* Corresponding Author's Email: gsmaha@annauniv.edu.

† Corresponding Author's Email: hemadharsana@gmail.com.

‡ Corresponding Author's Email: ksrividhyasaradha@gmail.com.

§ Corresponding Author's Email: ssk_pdy@yahoo.co.in.

In: Applications of Artificial Intelligence in the Healthcare Sector

Editors: Jyoti Prakash Patra and Yogesh Kumar Rathore

ISBN: 979-8-88697-502-4

7.1. Introduction

Topic models are widely used to represent the underlying theme of discussion in a given text. In document categorization, topic models are found to be very convincing. Topic models are unsupervised approaches to forming the set of top words of discussion within the given text. Every topic represents a perspective of discussion of ideas within the text and is represented by a set of word chains. These words have a particular order of representing the perspective within a given topic, irrespective of their physical ordering within the text. A word can repeat itself across topics to represent its share in establishing various topic perspectives. Such words are supported by a probability value that shows the contribution of the word to forming the respective topic perspective.

Every topic is also visualized with a topic probability score which represents the importance and share of the respective topic perspective among all topic perspectives in the underlying text. The membership words within a topic shall be fixed for all topic models as the word restriction would prevent the same words from appearing across numerous topics with the least probability share. However, the topic count is fixed for LDA-like models [1, 2] and is not fixed for generative topic models like HDP [3]. Though there is enough contribution in topic models and their variations and applications, all topic models proposed so far are representing unigrams and therefore unfit to represent scientific word topics. To fill this gap, this paper proposes the TnG-model for finding topic N-grams from scientific articles by following basic topic-modelling and n-gram analysis.

7.2. Literature Survey

Latent Semantic Indexing [4] followed by Latent Dirichlet Allocation [2] were the key contributors that started the topic modelling research. Hierarchical Dirichlet Process (HDP), Nested HDP [3], and Hierarchical Pitman Yor Dirichlet Language Model [5] were to name a few. Structural topic modelling (STM) is a notable improvement in probabilistic topic models. STM uses the Expectation-maximization technique to decide upon the topic distributions within a document [6]. Deep topic models [7, 8] learn topic distributions from the contextual sentences which are picked by an auto-encoder which is a Recurrent Neural Network with back propagation comprising three hidden layers. Neural Variational Document Model (NVDM) [9] uses multivariate Gaussian distribution as a prior distribution for representing latent spaces. LDA-VAE and Prod LDA are also derived on LDA using the Variational Auto Encoder technique [10]. Here multivariate Gaussian distribution is replaced by logistic normal distribution for latent space representations. The Local Latent Dirichlet Allocation (LLDA) model extracts words from overlapping windows. Therefore, unlike LDA, the topic of a word only affects the topic proportion of words which are in local proximity to the given word [11]. Earlier, Biterm topic models [12] used word co-occurrence patterns to produce topic distributions form a given short text.

Topic models (refer to Table 7.1) like LDA [2] and HDP [3] produce topics out of the given text data. Therefore, LDA [2] enforces the fixing of α for the number of topics and β for the number of words per topic perspective. Due to reasons mentioned in [7, 8], the fixing of words per topic and fixing of topics leads to varying topics yet, coherence is supported for these topic models. Chronologically CTM [1] (refer to Table 7.1) built upon concepts of LDA [2] results in better topics, as proved by the topic coherence measure. DLDA [7, 8] and DHDP [7, 8] provide better topic coherence compared to LDA [2] and HDP [3] with an improved set of contributing topics. However, the correlation of topics is lesser when compared to traditional CTM [1] despite fixing α and β values. Inspired by the concepts of Deep Topic Models [7, 8] this paper attempts to develop Deep Correlated Topic Models by incorporating Deep Stacked Sparse Au-to Encoder [8] for generating contributing sentences and feeding it via traditional CTM [1]. Correlated Topic models [1] utilize the correlation between topic proportions. These tend to use logistic normal distributions, unlike LDA word embedding are also attempted with correlated topic models [13]. Table 7.1 shows various topic models explored in the literature.

7.3. Modeling Topic N-Grams (TNG)

Topic N-gram Models (TnG) are supposed to utilize topic words from the underlying text and further aim to find whether the identified topic words are qualified to represent a popular n-gram. For this, the research article is subjected to N-gram identification. Basically, bi-grams and tri-grams are only examined since scientific words tend to spill across 2 and 3-gram entities only (See Figure 7.1). Proof to support this claim is reserved as future work.

Table 7.1. Various topic models proposed in the literature

S. No.	Topic Models	Year	Ref	S. No.	Topic Models	Year	Ref
1	Fuzzy topic modelling	2019	[14]	21	Gaussian dynamic topic model (GDTM)	2019	[36]
2	Prod LDA	2017	[15]	22	Knowledge-based Hierarchical Topic Model (KHTM)	2018	[37]
3	LDA - VAE	2017	[15]	23	Labelled LDA	2009	[38]
4	Dynamic Influential Model (DIM)	2010	[16, 17]	24	Hetero-Labelled LDA	2014	[39]
5	Bigram Topic Model	2006	[18]	25	Dirichlet multinomial model (DMM)	2000	[40]
6	HMM-LDA model	2005	[19]	26	Supervised LDA (SLDA)	2007	[41]
7	LDA	2003	[20-22]	27	Non-negative matrix factorization temporal topic model	2022	[42]
8	LDA Collocation (LDA-COL) model	2007	[23]	28	Archetypal LDA (A-LDA)	2022	[43]
9	Topical N-Grams (TNG) model	2007	[24, 25]	29	Correlated topic models (CTM)	2005	[44]
10	Digital topic modelling	2021	[26]	30	Neural Topic Models	2017	[45]
11	Structural Topic Model (STM)	2014	[27, 28]	31	Stick breaking construction	2012	[46, 47]
12	Adversarial-neural topic model	2019	[29]	32	Bidirectional Adversarial Topic (BAT) model	2020	[48]
13	LDA-VAE	2017	[30]	33	Topic embedding model - Correlated Topic Model	2017	[49]
14	Latent Event Model (LEM)	2014	[31]	34	Graph Attention Topic Network (GATON) for correlated topic modeling (GATON)	2020	[50]
15	Neural variational document model (NVDM)	2016	[32]	35	RoBERTa	2021	[51]
16	Nonparametric Topic Modelling	2020	[33]	36	Cross-perspective topic model	2012	[52]
17	infinite Topic Model with Variational Auto-Encoders (iTM-VAE)	2020	[33]	37	Gaussian LDA	2015	[53]
18	Hierarchical iTM-VAE (HiTM-VAE)	2020	[33]	38	Embedded topic model (ETM)	2020	[54]
19	HDP	2006	[34]	39	Contextualized Combined Topic model	2020	[55]
20	Stick-Breaking Variational Auto-Encoder	2017	[35]				

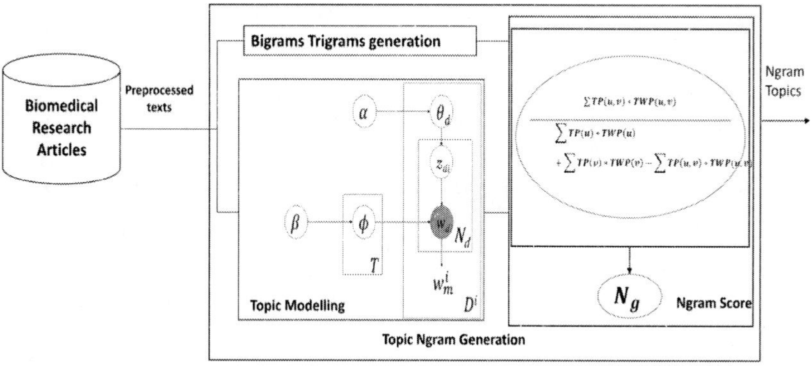

Figure 7.1. Topic N-gram modeling from text.

The N-grams identified are compared across topic models to examine if the n-gram or part of the n-gram is present as a prominent topic word. A single n-gram might be fully or partially present across various unigram topics. Based on the share of topic presence, the topic score is calculated for the topic N-gram. The methodology of topic scoring is explained as algorithm 1.

7.3.1. Algorithm 1: Topic N-Grams Identification

INPUT: Topic Modelled research articles
OUTPUT: Topic N-grams
Procedure:

1. Find all N-grams across articles of every year
2. Score every N-gram as

$$\text{Topic N-gram Score } N_g = \frac{\sum TP(u,v)*TWP(u,v)}{\sum TP(u)*TWP(u)+\sum TP(v)*TWP(v)-\sum TP(u,v)*TWP(u,v)} \quad (1)$$

where TP = Topic Probability of u, v
TWP = Topic word Probability of u, v

3. Filter and retain Top N-grams based on Score

Topic N-grams are used to identify the terms representative of the popular topics occurring across research articles of a huge chronological collection. The topic words may not be listed in the same order as they appeared in raw text. The topic N-gram score accounts for the same and identifies popular topics. Therefore, utilizing the basic N-gram identification and cross-examining it for the presence of any topic words leads to finding Topic N-grams. These Topic N-grams are regularly named entities as the essence of n-gram and topic perspective is bundled together over scientific word collections. However, labelling the entities is the next interesting step for complete utilization of the identified words for any text-based application and is out of the scope of the proposed work.

7.4. Result

The research articles in the Journal of Bio-medical Semantics years 2013 to 2020 are downloaded manually and labelled as the dataset. The research articles in pdf format were converted to text format and the spelling errors inserted during conversion were corrected. Also, the references to the articles were removed. The dataset has only the text portion of the research article and the figures if any were hereby eliminated in the process of conversion. This text-only dataset comprising 335 articles spanning the years 2013-2020 (refer to Table 7.2) is further sent for correlated deep topic modelling. LDA [2], HDP [9], DLDA [6], DHDP [6] and CTM [1] and DCTM [6] are assumed as baseline topic models for analysis. The dataset and the topics obtained for all topic models are available in GitHub. The top topic words and respective probabilities obtained across various topic models for unigrams and bigrams are tabulated in Table 7.3 and Table 7.4.

Table 7.2. Journal of Bio-medical Semantics (JBS) dataset

Year	Total articles Downloaded	Year	Total articles Downloaded
2013	52	2017	57
2014	57	2018	24
2015	41	2019	24
2016	66	2020	14

Table 7.3. Top topic word unigrams with probabilities across topic models (JBS 2020)

Topic Count	LDA		DLDA		HDP	
0	Disease	0.12789556384086	Publications	0.148449033498	Including	0.061261814087
	Method	0.05950221419334	events	0.074593797326	led	0.061261814087
	Words	0.03868684917688	methodologies	0.074593797326	approach	0.061261814087
	Subclass	0.02679235115647	features	0.074593797326	able	0.030783299356
	Classe	0.02381872758269	full	0.059502214193	fda	0.030783299356
	First	0.02381872758269	jh	0.035368949174	integrative	0.030783299356
	Method	0.02084510400891	solutions	0.074593797326	struggles	0.030783299356
	Classes	0.01787148043513	structured	0.045006264001	people	0.030783299356
	Neural	0.01489785593003	palliative	0.074593797326	applies	0.030783299356
	Syndrome	0.07459379732608	nlp	0.074593797326	accurate	0.030783299356
				0.074593797326		
1	System	0.04500626400113	text	0.018518518656	biomedical	0.149754345417
	Synonyms	0.03536894917488	clinical	0.018518518656	approaches	0.064302504062
	semantics terms	0.02894407138228	publications	0.028944071382	based	0.064302504062
	specific terms	0.02251919358968	language	0.018518518656	databases	0.042939543724
	mentions train class	0.02251919358968	processing	0.018518518656	inxight	0.021576587110
	refer	0.02251919358968	natural	0.018518518656	exceeds	0.021576587110
	classification	0.01930675655603	classification	0.061261814087	national	0.021576587110
	knowledge	0.01930675655603	rule based	0.018518518656	sharing	0.021576587110
		0.01930675655603	features knowledge	0.018518518656	derived	0.021576587110
		0.01930675655603		0.030783299356	genetic	0.021576587110
2	Classes	0.08352584391832	Overview	0.220043569803	Manual	0.049498438835
	Disease	0.03342703729867	Authors	0.220043569803	Databases	0.049498438835
	Use	0.02786050178110	Literature	0.220043569803	Neo	0.033053774386
	Within	0.02786050178110	stated	0.002178649185	Sciences	0.033053774386
	identify syndrome	0.01951070129871	commons	0.002178649185	Time	0.033053774386
	analysed	0.01951070129871	biomedical	0.002178649185	across	0.033053774386
	dictionary	0.01672743447124	Credit	0.002178649185	designation	0.033053774386

Table 7.3. (Continued)

Topic Count	LDA		DLDA		HDP	
2	model synonyms	0.01672743447124 0.01394416764378 0.01394416764378	Count Shatkay Feldman	0.002178649185	biomedical semantics amongst	0.033053774386 0.033053774386 0.016609109938
3	Word Text bacterial new medical ontology Journal Althubaiti Different Results	0.03593990951776 0.03593990951776 0.02748843282461 0.02748843282461 0.02748843282461 0.02326269261538 0.02326269261538 0.02114982344210 0.01903695426881 0.01903695426881	reproduction provide schroeder biomedical Credit Text Shatkay Feldman Mining 'literature'	0.281337052583 0.281337052583 0.281337052583 0.002785515272 0.002785515272 0.002785515272 0.002785515272 0.002785515272 0.002785515272 0.002785515272	Material semantically database nguyen source management Unii establishment format united	0.071992352604 0.048074625432 0.048074625432 0.048074625432 0.024156901985 0.024156901985 0.024156901985 0.024156901985 0.024156901985
4	Ontology anatomical Based system refers positive context Used Either ontologies	0.12884475290775 0.04715825244784 0.04401646181941 0.03773288428783 0.03144930675625 0.02202394045889 0.02202394045889 0.01888215169310 0.01574036292731 0.01259857416152	Licensed distribution percentage Source Access Medium Driver research Domain ontologies	0.105318039655 0.105318039655 0.105318039655 0.105318039655 0.105318039655 0.105318039655 0.105318039655 0.015740362927 0.001042752875 0.139021769165	Health Center Large Potential inheritance Studies Extracted Plain Genetic Analysis	0.139021769165 0.061873175203 0.061873175203 0.046443451195 0.046443451195 0.031013732776 0.031013732776 0.031013732776 0.031013732776 0.031013732776
	DHDP		CTM		DCTM	
0	Health ehr modelled Five	0.292151153087615 0.146802321076393 0.146802321076393 0.146802321076393	Disease Ontology medical Unique	0.153049170970 0.048744875937 0.041791252791 0.027884015813	Neural Ref guided Natural	0.051165148615 0.051165148615 0.051165148615 0.051165148615

Topic Count	DHDP		CTM		DCTM	
0	Sofa	0.146802321076393	Several	0.027884015813	Text	0.051165148615
	Based	0.001453488366678	Clinical	0.027884015813	Project	0.051165148615
	phenotypes	0.001453488366678	Study	0.020930394530	Thai	0.051165148615
	Dm	0.001453488366678	associations	0.020930394530	rule	0.051165148615
	Well	0.001453488366678	Neo	0.013976775109	Evaluation	0.051165148615
	including	0.001453488366678	biomedical	0.013976775109	Processing	0.051165148615
1	Case	0.144812673330307	Knowledge	0.106438897550	Natural	0.298219591379
	project	0.144812673330307	research	0.062636882066	Assessed	0.149851635098
	Based	0.072766572237014	Health	0.056379452347	classification	0.149851635098
	phenotypes	0.072766572237014	drugs	0.050122022628	language	0.149851635098
	structured	0.072766572237014	Use	0.037607159465	Semantic	0.001483679516
	clinical	0.072766572237014	database	0.037607159465	Neural	0.001483679516
	reasoning	0.072766572237014	curation	0.031349729746	Bigdata	0.001483679516
	Body	0.072046107379719	resources	0.025092298164	project	0.001483679516
	classification	0.072046107379719	Many	0.018834866583	run	0.001483679516
	Dm	0.072046107379719	management	0.012577435933	files	0.001483679516
2	queryable	0.171768695116043	integrative	0.054191194474	Based	0.013513512909
	structure	0.171768695116043	orphan	0.054191194474	publications	0.013513512909
	boolean	0.171768695116043	Support	0.054191194474	Natural	0.013513512909
	method	0.171768695116043	consumer	0.033894866704	Text	0.013513512909
	bmi	0.171768695116043	Fda	0.033894866704	Bigdata	0.013513512909
	Clinical	0.001700680237263	Article	0.033894866704	Project	0.013513512909
	research	0.001700680237263	potential	0.020363980904	Files	0.013513512909
	Based	0.001700680237263	integrated	0.020363980904	Keywords	0.013513512909
	phenotypes	0.001700680237263	curated	0.020363980904	Textfiles	0.013513512909
	dm	0.001700680237263	Well	0.020363980904		0.013513512909
3	example	0.1281725913286209	diseases	0.028277274221	Bigdata	0.270053476095
	compute	0.1281725913286209	regard	0.028277274221	Xml	0.270053476095
	calculation	0.1281725913286209	large	0.028277274221	tchechmedjiev	0.270053476095
	class	0.1281725913286209	designation	0.021225584670	publications	0.002673796610

Table 7.3. (Continued)

Topic Count	DHDP		CTM		DCTM	
3	selected	0.1281725913286209	zhu	0.021225584670	natural	0.002673796610
	surface	0.1281725913286209	developed	0.021225584670	Curate	0.002673796610
	medical	0.0012690355069935	based	0.021225584670	Project	0.002673796610
	Based	0.0012690355069935	established	0.014173895120	Run	0.002673796610
	phenotypes	0.0012690355069935	awareness	0.014173895120	Files	0.028277274221
	dm		Expert		keywords	0.021225584670
4	including	0.20344129204750	Graph	0.080605261027	Base	0.136363640427
	Dm	0.20344129204750	manual	0.028824580833	publications	0.136363640427
	correctly	0.10222671926021	Genetic	0.028824580833	Events	0.068521030247
	query	0.10222671926021	databases	0.023071171715	Author	0.068521030247
	input	0.10222671926021	scientific	0.023071171715	Barrett	0.068521030247
	selection	0.10222671926021	Graph	0.023071171715	Jahnke	0.068521030247
	economic	0.00101214565802	Center	0.017317760735	methodologies	0.068521030247
	clinical	0.00101214565802	Regard	0.017317760735	Files	0.068521030247
	research	0.00101214565802	different	0.017317760735	‘information’	0.028277274221
	Based		journal	0.017317760735	Sentinel	0.021225584670

Table 7.4. Top topic word bigrams with probabilities across topic models

JBS 2020 LDA BIGRAMS		JBS 2020 DLDA BIGRAMS	
Topic Weight	Bigrams	Topic Weight	Bigrams
0.0087593313137180360	[‘pathology,’ ‘report’]	0.04089043528418203	[‘machine,’ ‘learning’]
0.0173754179399180000	[‘bacterial,’ ‘infectious’]	0.23239546157785132	[‘original,’ ‘provide’]
0.0019172589402599305	[‘electronic,’ ‘health’]	0.06662455063355811	[‘dedication,’ ‘waiver’]
0.0039626255504892350	[‘feature,’ ‘sets’]	0.10863019551960552	[‘stated’, ‘credit’]
0.0008234240999851492	[‘influential,’ ‘authors’]	0.00248953382574827	[‘attribution’, ‘international’]
JBS 2020 HDP BIGRAMS		JBS 2020 DHDP BIGRAMS	
Topic Weight	Bigrams	Topic Weight	Bigrams
0.014036343743950887	[‘infectious,’ ‘disease’]	0.200183441339437220	[‘information’, ‘available’]
0.139058615240038700	[‘dental,’ ‘restoration’]	0.033210432308475810	[‘rare,’ ‘diseases’]
0.008562765156737530	[‘nursing,’ ‘notes’]	0.026929762182476225	[‘restoration,’ ‘procedure’]
0.017884428260395956	[‘training,’ ‘data’]	0.149855698032183800	[‘user,’ ‘credibility’]
0.763947855536370200	[‘restoration,’ ‘material’]	0.015470644544906062	[‘attribution,’ ‘international’]
JBS 2020 CTM BIGRAMS		JBS 2020 DCTM BIGRAMS	
Topic Weight	Bigrams	Topic Weight	Bigrams
0.007356262699638365	[‘free,’ ‘text’]	0.014954191840153909	[‘user,’ ‘expertise’]
0.0059641537615552406	[‘article,’ ‘included’]	0.030472870406900738	[‘subject,’ ‘domain’]
0.0014823737135257508	['bacterial', 'infectious']	0.073622614366847420	[‘credit,’ ‘original’]
0.0246285332474816200	[‘sparql,’ ‘query’]	0.115059183633060390	[‘natural,’ ‘language’]
0.0108966403371243260	[‘knowledge,’ ‘graph’]	0.015310808802753196	[‘language,’ ‘processing’]

The topic N-grams thus identified are evaluated using ROUGE-1 and ROUGE-2 metric (refer Table 7.5). It is evident that presence of topic bigrams is les sin compared to topic unigrams. However, there is a dare need to verify the same using alternative approaches. However, DCTM performs much better than other base-line topic models in identifying n-gram topic entities. Table 7.6-7.11 presents the precision, recall and F-score of baseline topic models when evaluated with ROUGE scores for topic unigrams and topic bigrams across SPACEE [56] generated entity names.

Table 7.5. ROUGE-1 and ROUGE-2 for TnG evaluation (JBS 2020) across baseline topic models

Baseline Models	Topic Unigrams - ROUGE 1			Topic Bigrams - ROUGE 2		
	Precision	Recall	F-score	Precision	Recall	F-score
LDA	0.79	0.41	0.54	0.09	0.05	0.06
HDP	0.79	0.56	0.66	0.10	0.06	0.07
DLDA	0.79	0.59	0.67	0.09	0.06	0.07
DHDP	0.81	0.68	0.74	0.10	0.06	0.08
CTM	0.82	0.70	0.75	0.10	0.07	0.08
DCTM	**0.85**	**0.74**	**0.79**	**0.10**	**0.07**	**0.08**

Table 7.6. ROUGE-1 and ROUGE-2 for TnG evaluation (JBS) across LDA

Year	Topic Unigrams - ROUGE 1			Topic Bigrams - ROUGE 2		
	Precision	Recall	F-score	Precision	Recall	F-score
2020	0.79	0.41	0.54	0.09	0.05	0.06
2019	0.79	0.42	0.55	0.10	0.06	0.07
2018	0.78	0.42	0.54	0.10	0.05	0.07
2017	0.79	0.43	0.56	0.13	0.07	0.09
2016	0.59	0.38	0.46	0.07	0.05	0.06
2015	0.72	0.17	0.27	0.13	0.03	0.05
2014	0.56	0.42	0.48	0.07	0.06	0.06
2013	0.70	0.26	0.38	0.11	0.04	0.06

Table 7.7. ROUGE-1 and ROUGE-2 for TnG evaluation (JBS) across DLDA

Year	Topic Unigrams - ROUGE 1			Topic Bigrams - ROUGE 2		
	Precision	Recall	F-score	Precision	Recall	F-score
2020	0.790	0.587	0.673	0.094	0.057	0.071
2019	0.789	0.587	0.673	0.095	0.057	0.071
2018	0.772	0.575	0.660	0.096	0.058	0.072
2017	0.771	0.570	0.656	0.097	0.058	0.073
2016	0.765	0.565	0.650	0.097	0.056	0.071
2015	0.760	0.560	0.645	0.096	0.055	0.070
2014	0.755	0.551	0.637	0.095	0.054	0.069
2013	0.743	0.544	0.629	0.094	0.054	0.069

For most of the years, DCTM performs best when compared to other baseline models for Topic unigrams. However, HDP performs marginally higher than all other baseline models for Topic bigrams. The reason is that HDP is more generative in identifying topic words and topic perspectives such that all possible perspectives are analyzed automatically and the complete topic essence of the underlying text is obtained. For the same reason, HDP produces more topic perspectives though per topic word count only shall be restricted. Therefore, the file size becomes higher than any other baseline models as more topics are present comparatively. Therefore, for the years 2014 and 2015 (Table 7.8) the article sizes were higher thereby producing bulkier topic files and it was hard to run the HDP to completion using the same configuration of the laptop. Also, topic bigrams are lesser compared to topic unigrams (refer to Table 7.12) which was a clear indication in ROUGE 2 scores across almost all the baseline models.

Table 7.8. ROUGE-1 and ROUGE-2 for TnG evaluation (JBS) across HDP

Year	Topic Unigrams - ROUGE 1			Topic Bigrams - ROUGE 2		
	Precision	Recall	F-score	Precision	Recall	F-score
2020	0.788	0.561	0.655	0.095	0.060	0.074
2019	0.790	0.558	0.654	**0.101**	0.058	0.074
2018	0.788	0.550	0.647	**0.101**	0.058	0.073
2017	0.778	0.534	0.633	**0.102**	0.057	0.073
2016	0.766	0.538	0.632	**0.103**	0.055	0.071
2013	0.700	0.330	0.448	**0.105**	0.050	0.067

Table 7.9. ROUGE-1 and ROUGE-2 for TnG evaluation (JBS) across DHDP

Year	Topic Unigrams - ROUGE 1			Topic Bigrams - ROUGE 2		
	Precision	Recall	F-score	Precision	Recall	F-score
2020	0.807	0.681	0.739	0.096	0.063	0.076
2019	0.807	0.680	0.738	0.096	0.063	0.076
2018	0.807	0.680	0.738	0.096	0.064	0.077
2017	0.806	0.681	0.738	0.098	0.065	0.078
2016	0.806	0.674	0.734	0.098	0.065	0.078
2015	0.805	0.671	0.732	0.097	0.064	0.077
2014	0.805	0.670	0.731	0.097	0.064	0.077
2013	0.805	0.658	0.724	0.096	0.064	0.077

Table 7.10. ROUGE-1 and ROUGE-2 for TnG evaluation (JBS) across CTM

Year	Topic Unigrams - ROUGE 1			Topic Bigrams - ROUGE 2		
	Precision	Recall	F-score	Precision	Recall	F-score
2020	0.816	0.701	0.754	0.097	0.069	0.080
2019	0.815	0.702	0.754	0.097	0.069	0.081
2018	0.816	0.701	0.754	0.096	0.068	0.080
2017	0.814	0.701	0.753	0.095	0.067	0.079
2016	0.815	0.703	0.755	0.097	0.069	0.081
2015	0.814	0.702	0.754	0.096	0.068	0.080
2014	0.810	0.700	0.751	0.094	0.066	0.078
2013	0.811	0.699	0.751	0.094	0.065	0.077

Table 7.11. ROUGE-1 and ROUGE-2 for TnG evaluation (JBS) across DCTM

Year	Topic Unigrams - ROUGE 1			Topic Bigrams - ROUGE 2		
	Precision	Recall	F-score	Precision	Recall	F-score
2020	**0.851**	0.741	0.792	**0.098**	0.073	0.083
2019	**0.851**	0.740	0.791	0.098	0.073	0.084
2018	**0.852**	0.740	0.792	0.098	0.072	0.083
2017	**0.853**	0.739	0.792	0.097	0.073	0.083
2016	**0.853**	0.740	0.793	0.098	0.073	0.083
2015	**0.851**	0.736	0.790	0.098	0.073	0.083
2014	**0.849**	0.735	0.788	0.096	0.072	0.082
2013	**0.845**	0.730	0.784	0.096	0.072	0.082

Table 7.12. Unigram entities and bigram entities of JBS according to SPACEE

	# Unigram Entities	# Bigram Entities
2013	21653	13741
2014	25789	17673
2015	14515	12421
2016	38456	15115
2017	23564	21286
2018	9573	7235
2019	10460	8678
2020	7001	5017

Conclusion

This paper proposes the identification of topic n-grams from scientific research articles by fusion approach. The proposed approach of combining basic topic modelling and n-gram analysis over the given text generates topic unigrams of almost close to 85%. However, identification of topic bigrams and topic trigrams is of utmost importance as the scientific articles are from the biomedical discipline. Therefore, a better treatment of generated topics is essential for measuring topic bigrams and topic trigrams.

References

[1] Blei, D. M., Lafferty, J. D. A correlated topic model of science, *The Annals of Applied Statistics,* 1(1), 17-35 (2007).

[2] Blei, David M. Probabilistic topic models. *Communications of the ACM*, 55(4):77-84 (2012).

[3] Paisley, John, Chong, Wang, Blei, D. M., Michael Jordan. Nested hierarchical Dirichlet processes, *IEEE Transactions on Pattern Analysis and Machine Intelligence*, vol. 37, no. 2, pp. 256-270 (2015).

[4] Hofmann, T. Probabilistic latent semantic indexing, Article presented at the *Proceedings of the 22nd annual international ACM SIGIR conference on Research and development in information retrieval*, pp. 14. (1999).

[5] Chien, Jen-Tzung. Hierarchical Pitman-Yor-Dirichlet language model, *IEEE Transactions on Audio, Speech, and Language Processing*, vol. 23, no. 8, pp. 1259-1272(2015).

[6] Roberts, M. E., Stewart, B. M., Tingley, D. STM An r package for structural topic models. *Journal of Statistical Software*, 91(1), 1-40. https://doi.org/10.18637/ jss.v091.i02 (2019).

[7] Mahalakshmi, G. S., Hemadharsana, S., Muthuselvi, G., & Sendhilkumar, S. Learning Deep Topics of Interest. In *International Conference on Computational Vision and Bio Inspired Computing* (pp. 1517-1532). Springer, Cham. (2018, November).

[8] MuthuSelvi, G., Mahalakshmi, G. S., Sendhilkumar, S., Vijayakumar, Yongxin Zhu, Victor Chang. Sustainable Computing Based Deep Learning Framework for Writing Research Manuscripts, *IEEE Transactions on Sustainable Computing*, ISSN: 2377-3782 (2018).

[9] Miao, Yishu, Lei Yu, Phil Blunsom. Neural variational inference for text processing, In *International conference on machine learning*, pp. 1727-1736. PMLR (2016).

[10] Srivastava, A, Sutton, C. Autoencoding variational inference for topic models. 5th *international conference on learning representations (ICLR),* Toulon, France (2017).

[11] Rahimi, M., Zahedi, M., Mashayekhi, H. A Probabilistic Topic Model based on Short Distance Cooccurrences. *Expert Systems with Applications*, 116518(2022).

[12] Cheng, X., Yan, X., Lan, Y. Guo, J. Btm: Topic modeling over short texts, *IEEE Transactions on Knowledge and Data Engineering,* 26(12), pp. 2928-2941 (2014).

[13] Xun, G., Li, Y., Zhao, W. X., Gao, J., Zhang, A. A correlated topic model using word embeddings, In *IJCAI* pp. 4207-4213 (2017, August).

[14] Rashid, J., Shah, S. M. A., & Irtaza, A. (2019). Fuzzy topic modeling approach for text mining over short text. *Information Processing & Management*, 56(6), Article 102060. https://doi.org/10.1016/j.ipm.2019.102060.

[15] Srivastava, C. Sutton, Autoencoding variational inference for topic models, In *International Conference on Learning Representations*, 2017.

[16] Gerrish, S. M., Blei, D. M., 2010. A language-based approach to measuring scholarly impact. *Proceedings of the 27th International Conference on Machine Learning. Omni-press,* pp. 375-382.

[17] Xu, S., Hao, L., Yang, G., Lu, K., & An, X. (2021). A topic models based framework for detecting and forecasting emerging technologies. *Technological Forecasting and Social Change*, 162, 120366.

[18] Wallach, H. M., 2006. Topic modeling: Beyond bag-of-words. Proceedings of the 23rd *International Conference on Machine Learning*. pp. 977-984. https://doi.org/10. 1145/1143844.1143967.

[19] Griffiths, T. L., Steyvers, M., Blei, D. M., Tenenbaum, J. B., 2005. Integrating topics and syntax. In: Saul, L. K., Weiss, Y., Bottou, L. (Eds.), *Advances in Neural Information Processing Systems 17*. MIT Press, Cambridge, MA, pp. 537-544.

[20] Blei, D. M., Ng, A. Y., Jordan, M. I., 2003. Latent Dirichlet allocation. *J. Mach. Learn. Res*. 3 (Jan), 993-1022.

[21] Blei, D. M., 2012. Probabilistic topic models. Commun. *ACM* 55 (4), 77-84. https://doi.org/10.1145/2133806.2133826.

[22] Jelodar, H., Wang, Y., Yuan, C., Feng, X., Jiang, X., 2019. Latent Dirichlet Allocation (LDA) and topic modeling: models, applications, a survey. *Multimed. Tool. Appl*. 78 (11), 15169-15211.

[23] Griffiths, T. L., Steyvers, M., Tenenbaum, J. B., 2007. Topics in semantic representation. *Psychol. Rev*. 114 (2), 211-244. https://doi.org/10.1037/0033-295X.114.2.211.

[24] Wang, X., McCallum, A., Wei, X., 2007. Topical n-grams: Phrase and topic discovery, with an application to information retrieval. *Proceedings of the 7th IEEE International Conference on Data Mining*. IEEE Computer Society, Washington, DC, USA, pp. 697-702. https://doi.org/10.1109/ICDM.2007.86.

[25] Xu, S., Hao, L., Yang, G., Lu, K., & An, X. (2021). A topic models based framework for detecting and forecasting emerging technologies. *Technological Forecasting and Social Change,* 162, 120366.

[26] Shah, A. M., Yan, X., Tariq, S., & Ali, M. (2021). What patients like or dislike in phy-sicians: Analyzing drivers of patient satisfaction and dissatisfaction using a digital topic modeling approach. *Information Processing & Management*, 58(3), 102516.

[27] Roberts, M. E., Stewart, B. M., Tingley, D., Lucas, C., Leder-Luis, J., Gadarian, S. K., Albertson, B., & Rand, D. G. (2014). Structural Topic Models for open-ended survey responses. *American Journal of Political Science*, 58(4), 1064-1082.

[28] Sharma, A., Rana, N. P., & Nunkoo, R. (2021). Fifty years of information management research: A conceptual structure analysis using structural topic modeling. *International Journal of Information Management*, 58, 102316.

[29] Wang, R., Zhou, D., & He, Y. (2019). Atm: Adversarial-neural topic model. *Information Processing & Management*, 56(6), 102098.

[30] Srivastava, A., & Sutton, C. (2017). Autoencoding variational inference for topic models. 5th *international conference on learning representations (ICLR)*, Toulon, France.

[31] Zhou, D., Chen, L., & He, Y. (2014). A simple Bayesian modelling approach to event extraction from twitter. *Proceedings of the 52nd annual meeting of the 390 association for computational linguistics, ACL* 2014, Vol. 2, Baltimore, Maryland, USA700-705. https://doi.org/10.3115/v1/p14-2114.

[32] Miao, Y., Yu, L., & Blunsom, P. (2016). Neural variational inference for text processing. *Proceedings of the 33rd international conference on machine learning*, New York, NY, USA1727-1736.

[33] Ning, X., Zheng, Y., Jiang, Z., Wang, Y., Yang, H., Huang, J., & Zhao, P. (2020). Nonparametric topic modeling with neural inference. *Neurocomputing*, 399, 296-306.

[34] M. J. B. Yee Whye Teh Michael I. Jordan, D. M. Blei, Hierarchical dirichlet processes, *J. Am. Stat. Assoc.* 101 (476) (2006) 1566-1581.

[35] E. Nalisnick, P. Smyth, Stick-breaking variational autoencoders, In *International Conference on Learning Representations*, 2017.

[36] Li, Q., Liu, L., Xu, M., Wu, B., & Xiao, Y. (2019). GDTM: A Gaussian Dynamic Topic Model for Forwarding Prediction under Complex Mechanisms. *IEEE Transactions on Computational Social Systems,* 6(2), 338-349. https://doi.org/10.1109/TCSS.2019.2900299.

[37] Xu, Y., Yin, J., Huang, J., & Yin, Y. (2018). Hierarchical topic modeling with automatic knowledge mining. *Expert Systems with Applications*, 103, 106-117. https://doi.org/10.1016/j.eswa.2018.03.008.

[38] Ramage, D., Hall, D., Nallapati, R., & Manning, C. D. (2009). Labeled LDA: A supervised topic model for credit attribution in multi-labeled corpora. EMNLP 2009 - *Proceedings of the 2009 Conference on Empirical Methods in Natural Language Processing: A Meeting of SIGDAT, a Special Interest Group of ACL, Held in Conjunction with ACL-IJCNLP* 2009, August, 248-256.

[39] Kang, D., Park, Y., & Chari, S. N. (2014). Hetero-labeled LDA: A partially supervised topic model with heterogeneous labels. *Lecture Notes in Computer Science (Including Subseries Lecture Notes in Artificial Intelligence and Lecture Notes in Bioinformatics), 8724 LNAI* (PART 1), 640-655. https://doi.org/10.1007/978-3-662-44848-9_41.

[40] Thrun, S., Mitchell, T. O. M., Nigam, K., & McCallum, A. (2000). Text classification from labeled and unlabeled documents using EM. *Machine Learning*, 34, 103-134. http: //www.springerlink.com/index/p4324q3673265225.pdf.

[41] Blei, D. M., & McAuliffe, J. D. (2007). Supervised topic models. *Advances in Neural Information Processing Systems*, 121-128. http://papers.nips.cc/paper/3328-super vised-topic-models.

[42] Meaney, C., Escobar, M., Moineddin, R., Stukel, T. A., Kalia, S., Aliarzadeh, B., & Greiver, M. (2022). Non-negative matrix factorization temporal topic models and clinical text data identify COVID-19 pandemic effects on primary healthcare and community health in Toronto, Canada. *Journal of Biomedical Informatics*, 128, 104034.

[43] Steuber, F., Schneider, S., & Schoenfeld, M. (2022). Embedding Semantic Anchors to Guide Topic Models on Short Text Corpora. *Big Data Research*, 27, 100293.

[44] D. M. Blei, J. D. Lafferty, Correlated topic models, In *Proceedings of the 18th Interna-tional Conference on Neural Information Processing Systems*, MIT Press, Cambridge, MA, USA, 2005, pp. 147-154.

[45] Miao, Y., Grefenstette, E., & Blunsom, P. (2017, July). Discovering discrete latent topics with neural variational inference. In *International Conference on Machine Learning* (pp. 2410-2419). PMLR.

[46] Miao, Y., Grefenstette, E., & Blunsom, P. (2017, July). Discovering discrete latent topics with neural variational inference. In *International Conference on Machine Learning* (pp. 2410-2419). PMLR.

[47] Khan, Mohammad Emtiyaz, Mohamed, Shakir, Marlin, Benjamin M, and Murphy, Kevin P. A stick-breaking likelihood for categorical data analysis with latent Gaussian models. In *Proceedings of AISTATS*, 2012.

[48] Wang, R., Hu, X., Zhou, D., He, Y., Xiong, Y., Ye, C., & Xu, H. (2020). *Neural topic modeling with bidirectional adversarial training*. arXiv preprint arXiv:2004.12331.

[49] Junxian He, Zhiting Hu, Taylor Berg-Kirkpatrick, Ying Huang, and Eric P Xing. 2017. Efficient correlated topic modeling with topic embedding. In *SIGKDD*. 225-233.

[50] Yang, Liang, Fan Wu, Junhua Gu, Chuan Wang, Xiaochun Cao, Di Jin, and Yuanfang Guo. "Graph attention topic modeling network." In *Proceedings of The Web Conference* 2020, pp. 144-154. 2020.

[51] Ghasiya, P., & Okamura, K. (2021). Investigating COVID-19 news across four nations: a topic modeling and sentiment analysis approach. *IEEE Access*, 9, 36645-36656.

[52] Fang, Y., Si, L., Somasundaram, N., & Yu, Z. (2012) Mining contrastive opinions on political texts using cross-perspective topic model. In: *Proceedings of the fifth ACM international conference on web search and data mining*. ACM.

[53] Das, R., Zaheer, M., & Dyer, C. (2015, July). Gaussian LDA for topic models with word embeddings. In Proceedings of the 53rd Annual Meeting of the Association for Computational Linguistics and the 7th *International Joint Conference on Natural Language Processing* (Volume 1: Long Papers) (pp. 795-804).

[54] Dieng, A. B., Ruiz, F. J., & Blei, D. M. (2020). Topic modeling in embedding spaces. *Transactions of the Association for Computational Linguistics*, 8, 439-453.

[55] Bianchi, F., Terragni, S., & Hovy, D. (2020). *Pre-training is a hot topic: Contextualized document embeddings improve topic coherence*. arXiv preprint arXiv:2004.03974.

[56] Honnibal, M., & Montani, I. (2017). *spaCy 2: Natural language understanding with Bloom embeddings, convolutional neural networks and incremental parsing*.

Chapter 8

A Chronic Disease Diagnosis Model for Smart Healthcare Systems Enabled by Artificial Intelligence and the Internet of Things

M. S. Guru Prasad[1,*], Pranav More[2,†], Sharon Christa[1,‡] and M. Anand kumar[3,§]

[1]Department of Computer Science and Engineering, Graphic Era (Deemed to be University), Dehradun, India
[2]School of Technology Management and Engineering, SVKM's NMIMS University, Navi Mumbai, India
[3]Department of Computer Applications, Graphic Era (Deemed to be University), Dehradun, India

Abstract

Smart healthcare is the result of recent advances in Artificial Intelligence (AI), Big Data, and the Internet of Things (IoT). The quality of healthcare can be improved by adopting vital new technology. The healthcare industry stands to gain from the convergence of Artificial Intelligence and IoT in numerous ways. The current study effort presents a chronic disease diagnosis model for a smart healthcare system that is based on the convergence of Artificial Intelligence and the Internet of Things. Diagnosing an illness refers to the process of identifying a health problem, disease, ailment, or other condition that a person may be experiencing. It is possible that disease diagnosis will be a simple chore at times, while others may be a little more difficult. However, even if

[*] Corresponding Author's Email: guru0927@gmail.com.
[†] Corresponding Author's Email: pranavmore2530@gmail.com.
[‡] Corresponding Author's Email: sharonchrista.cse@geu.ac.in.
[§] Corresponding Author's Email: anandkumar@geu.ac.in.

In: Applications of Artificial Intelligence in the Healthcare Sector
Editors: Jyoti Prakash Patra and Yogesh Kumar Rathore
ISBN: 979-8-88697-502-4

there are abundant data sets accessible, there is a lack of tools that are good at identifying patterns and making predictions. Diagnosing an illness with traditional procedures is time-consuming and prone to errors because they are done manually. Developing a chronic disease detection model that includes Artificial Intelligence and Internet of Things convergence approaches is the major objective of our work. The application of Artificial Intelligence (AI) prediction approaches allows for the use of auto diagnostics, which reduces the number of detection mistakes compared to the use of solely human expertise. The proposed study consists of several steps, including data collection, preprocessing, classification, and parameter adjustment, among others. Wearables and sensors, which are part of the Internet of Things, allow for smooth data collection, while artificial intelligence algorithms make use of the data in disease detection. A major purpose of the proposed study is to offer significant new information about various artificial intelligence approaches in the medical area, both current and historical, that are now being employed in today's medical research, specifically in the prediction of heart and brain disease as well as liver and kidney disease. Finally, based on a set of open difficulties and challenges, the study suggests several directions for future research into artificial intelligence-based diagnostics systems.

Keywords: smart health, artificial intelligence, big data, internet of things, chronic disease, diagnosis, health care prediction

8.1. Introduction

About 22 percent of the population will be 60 or older by 2050, which means that the number of people with chronic conditions and health-related emergencies will increase, putting a greater strain on the healthcare system. There are fewer healthcare professionals to meet the rising demand because of a decrease in the working-age population. In addition, the cost of health care, pharmaceuticals, and medical gadgets continue to rise, making it increasingly difficult for the average citizen to fund such charges as the demand for additional caregivers and healthcare facilities grows [1]. When all three of these factors are taken into consideration, it becomes clear that more affordable, more accessible, and higher-quality health care is needed. Artificial intelligence, smart and tiny sensors, and other cutting-edge technology are excellent candidates for this type of circumstance because they may be used to deliver technical solutions to a wide range of people at an inexpensive cost without losing the quality of care.

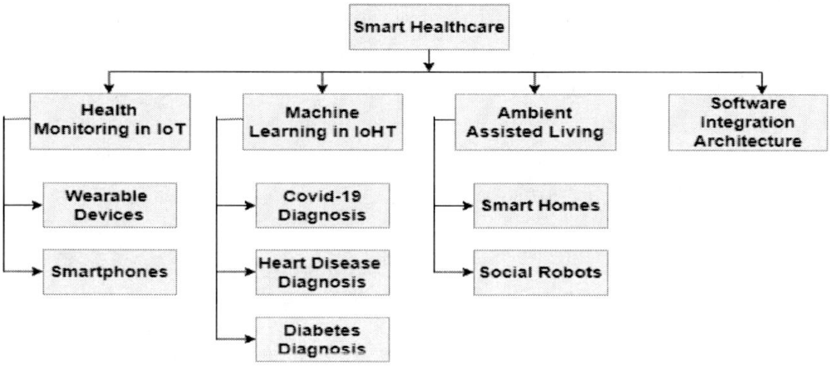

Figure 8.1. The overall process of the smart healthcare systems.

Figure 8.1 depicts the overall process of the smart healthcare systems that were under consideration. The thorough analysis of smart healthcare systems is separated into four primary areas. The Internet of Things (IoT) has gained in popularity in recent years. Advancements in technology and information transmission speeds have made it possible for large amounts of data to be communicated rapidly and easily. Big data analytics [2], as well as cloud technologies [3], have emerging markets and opportunities for IoT in meaningful analysis and simulation modelling. The healthcare industry has a lot to look forward to, especially with the advancements in IoT technology for real-time and continuous healthcare that were previously addressed. The Internet of Health Things (IoHT) [4] or the Internet of Medical Things (IoMT) [5] is a growing field that has the potential to transform how healthcare is delivered. The approach taken in both research and practice can be classified into a few basic types. Smart sensors are first integrated into the IoMT ecosystem, utilizing wearable technology [6] and mobile apps such as those provided by [7] in order to monitor health vitals. When smart sensors collect data, machine learning techniques can be used to evaluate and provide actionable insights, such as the ability to anticipate diseases [8]. Numerous algorithms are used to take care of chronic diseases such as diabetes [9], as well as track changes in the patient's condition [10].

One of the most important factors driving the adoption of smart healthcare is the rising proportion of elderly people in nations throughout the world. The ambient assisted living movement, as a result, focuses on designing surroundings for older individuals that use smart healthcare technologies to provide better care without the need for human interaction. Because nearly 90% of older people prefer to live in their own homes, many solutions, such as those presented in [11], are based on smart home technologies. Three user studies [12-15] found that including artificial agents in the functioning of interpersonal relationships with the user is crucial for providing both psychological and physical assistance to older people. There have been several studies on the use of robotic agents in senior care [16-19], and some have proposed going one step further by combining autonomous agents in ambient assisted living (AAL) environments with other sensing devices [20-22]. To integrate a large number of sensors, actuators, and user interfaces, extensive work on scalability and customization to different user demands must be done prior to deployment. In studies like [23, 24], and [25], people have tried to write down a lot of different architectures so that they can get around this problem and make integrated smart healthcare systems.

Fog and edge computing are crucial in smart healthcare because they lower the computational load on cloud servers while simultaneously ensuring continuous medical services with the shortest possible response times. Fog and edge computing, as a result of its decentralization, provides connectivity between end devices and the cloud in terms of computing power, storage, and networking. Cloud computing is all about shifting the burden of data centre operations onto fog nodes strategically located at the network's perimeter. When installed at the network's edge, fog devices execute tasks that allow for high data transmission rates and rapid response times. Data is typically analyzed on a cloud server in healthcare systems, which leads to high latency and bandwidth requirements when dealing with large amounts of information. It is possible to treat patients in real-time using a fog-enabled healthcare framework that gathers and processes information through the Internet of Things (IoT) devices in the fog layer [26]. As opposed to central processing units, edge computing places computers and data storage at the place where data is acquired and analyzed. An edge server for real-time data processing and a sensor network are both included in this architecture. Thanks to the Internet of Things devices and 6G networks, it is possible to create sophisticated and real-time healthcare apps that are both energy-efficient and latency-aware. Edge computing approaches can increase the reliability and responsiveness of decentralized applications, such as healthcare. A smart healthcare platform's ability to map IoT devices and sensors, as well as to manage resources, is critical [27].

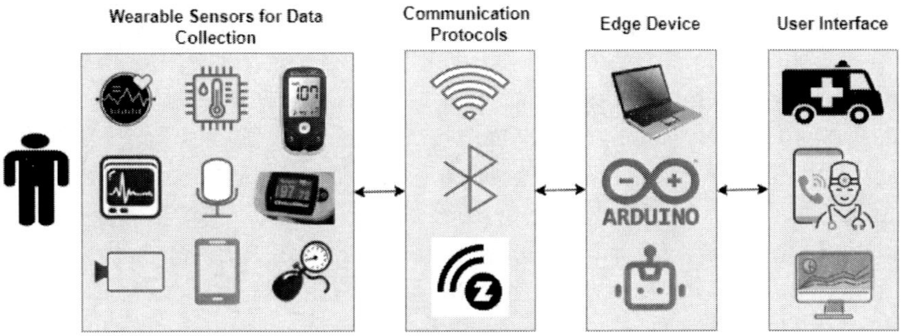

Figure 8.2. A wearable health monitoring system's general pipeline.

Figure 8.2 depicts a high-level overview of a wearable health monitoring system. Massive volumes of e-health data are being generated on a daily basis as a result of the rapid growth of the Internet of Things devices. It is essential to enhance data security. Applying blockchain technology to smart healthcare could address data sharing, security, and privacy concerns [28]. Safe blocks of data must be connected together with the use of an encrypted data record in order for blockchain technology to work. A centralized administrator isn't needed because the data is stored in synchronized database systems that were rebuilt from the ground up. Because it is a distributed system spread throughout a network, it provides system security in addition to good data collection. As a result of the many investigations into how to keep medical data safe, some interesting architectures for smart health care that employs blockchain technology to do just that can be found in articles [29-33]. Using the consortium blockchain and cryptographic primitives, the authors of [34] propose a mechanism for securely sharing data in the healthcare industry. Using blockchain technology, [35] proposes a plan for the long-term preservation of electronic health data, in which cryptographic techniques are employed to safeguard the privacy of patients. Using order-preserving encryption methods, a telemedicine system architecture known as BMPLS was developed [36] for the purpose of providing multi-level location privacy.

8.2. Literature Survey

We are seeing the rise of artificial intelligence (AI) in business and society as well as its use in healthcare. Many areas of patient care and administrative operations in healthcare providers, insurance companies, and the pharmaceutical industry could be altered by these technologies. Many studies have already demonstrated that artificial intelligence (AI) can outperform or even outperform humans when it comes to critical healthcare tasks like disease diagnosis [37]. By seeing deadly tumors before radiologists can, algorithms are instructing researchers on how to assemble cohorts for costly clinical studies. For many years to come, AI will not be able to replace humans in large medical processes, such as clinical trials. The term "artificial intelligence" refers to a group of interconnected technologies rather than a single entity [38]. These technologies are directly useful to the healthcare industry, but the procedures and duties that they enable are extremely diverse. The following topics provide an in-depth look at a few of the most essential AI technologies for the healthcare business.

8.2.1. Machine Learning: Neural Networks and Deep Learning

Machine learning is a statistical approach to fitting models to data and learning through the training of models with data. Deloitte surveyed 1,100 US managers whose organizations were already studying artificial intelligence and found that 63% of the companies asked were employing machine learning in their daily operations [39]. Many AI methods are built on top of this technology, which can be used in many different ways. A direct effect of this is that precision medicine, which entails predicting which treatment techniques are most likely to work for a given patient, is the most commonly encountered application of traditional machine learning in healthcare. The use of a training dataset in machine learning and precision medicine is typical practice in order to anticipate the outcome of a given experiment.

This advanced kind of machine learning, neural networks, has been around since the 1960s and has been used in healthcare research for decades. This approach to issue resolution takes into account all of the factors or "features" that relate inputs to outputs. Brain function has been compared to neuronal signal processing, but the resemblance is inadequate. The most difficult sort of machine learning is deep learning, which uses neural network models with multiple levels of characteristics or variables to predict outcomes. Using today's GPU and cloud-based architectures, which are faster than in the past, these models may expose hidden aspects. Deep learning is used a lot in the healthcare industry to look for tumors that might be cancerous in radiographs. In the field of deep learning, radiomics, or the finding of clinically relevant signals in visual input beyond what the human eye can see, is fast gaining ground. Radiomics and deep learning are most commonly found in oncology-focused image analysis. Computer-aided detection (CAD) systems for image analysis appear to be more accurate when they are combined with these technologies [40]. Deep learning is a subset of natural language processing (NLP), which particularly incorporates speech recognition. Observers of a deep learning model are often baffled as to what a particular feature means. Because of this, it may be impossible or very hard to understand the model's output.

8.2.2. Natural Language Processing

As far back as the 1950s, the goal of AI researchers has been to make sense of human language. Language-related applications of NLP include speech recognition, text analysis, and translation. Statistical and semantic NLP are two of the most common methodologies. The accuracy of recognition has recently improved thanks to statistical NLP, which is built on machine learning. It is necessary to have a huge corpus of language to learn from [41]. When it comes to clinical documentation and published research, NLP is most commonly used for its ability to automatically create, understand, and classify it. Unstructured clinical notes can be analyzed by NLP systems to prepare reports, record patient encounters, and perform conversational AI.

8.2.3. Rule-Based Expert Systems

The main AI technique in the 1980s was based on a set of "if-then" principles, which were widely used commercially at the time. During the last few decades, they have been widely employed in healthcare for "healthcare decision assistance" purposes, and they are still in use today. Typically, EHR providers include a system of regulations with their systems [42]. To build a set of rules in a certain area of expertise. They are simple to comprehend and effective up to a point. However, when the number of rules grows too large and the rules start to conflict with one another, the system becomes unmanageable and useless. In healthcare, data-driven and machine-learning algorithms are progressively displacing traditional approaches.

8.2.4. Physical Robots

Physical robots are becoming increasingly well-known thanks to the annual installation of more than 1 million mobile automation around the world. Workers at factories and warehouses are responsible for pre-defining duties, such as lifting and moving, cutting and assembling, or moving items to patients in hospitals. It has become easier for robots to be taught by guiding people through the desired action, as was formerly the case. As more artificial intelligence is added to their "brains," they are likewise becoming more intelligent. In the future, it looks likely that physical robots will benefit from the same advances in artificial intelligence that have been made in other fields. In 2000, the FDA granted permission for surgical robots to be used on humans in the United States. These devices provide surgeons with "superpowers" by improving their vision, allowing them to perform more precise incisions with less trauma, suture wounds more quickly, and more [43]. In contrast, human surgeons are still in charge of making critical decisions. Robotic surgery is commonly used to do gynaecological, prostate, and head and neck surgeries, among other treatments.

8.3. A Comparison of IoMT Monitoring Solutions

Several smart health monitoring IoT ideas have appeared in the last decade. IoT-based health care systems have a long history, and several interesting studies have been selected to illustrate this history. These studies range from early monitoring solutions that used only edge nodes for cognitive activities

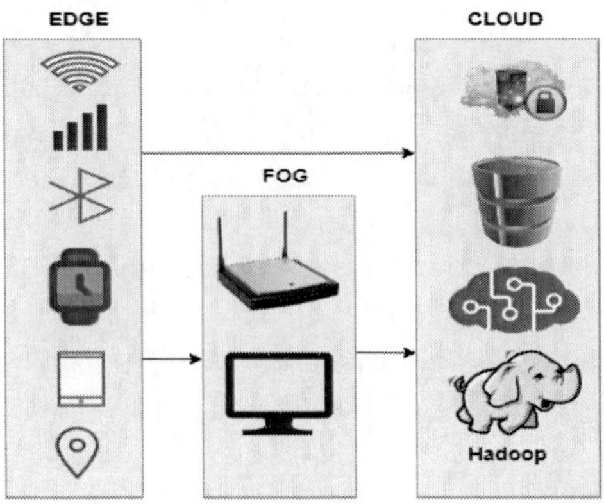

Figure 8.3. An IoMT system's three-tier architecture.

to more modern models that use cooperative edge/fog computing and enable the use of Edge Machine Learning. Researchers examined a wide range of health-related topics by utilizing various smart health system devices and sensors (e.g., bodily functions as well as speech, movement, posture, and skin diseases). Based on the problems they were trying to address, we categorized the contributions (See Figure 8.3).

8.3.1. Physiological Parameter Analysis

Systems that use physiological data as health indicators could be made to help people avoid dangerous situations that could cause accidents. WBSN monitoring of heart rate and mobility rate in people's homes is an interesting contribution from Magana Espinoza et al. [42]. The edge node can send an alarm to family members or professionals via smartphone in the event of a sudden change in measured data. According to Villarrubia et al., ECG data can be used to monitor patients at home and evaluate their heart health. An easy-to-use TV interface is available for patients to communicate with the system. When it comes to fever diagnosis, explores the use of the Bluemix cloud platform to acquire pharmacological data and allows clinicians to view the results of their analysis through the IBM Watson IoT platform, while [43] offers a case study on fever diagnosis using an Arduino microcontroller that helps in monitoring the patient's temperature. Both of these studies focus on fever diagnosis. U. Satija et al. [44] propose an Internet of Things-based real-time ECG telemetry system. Quality assessment algorithms have been installed on an Android smartphone for the first time, allowing authentic monitoring of the algorithms' performance. The authors show the approach's utility through a variety of physical exercises. A multimodal activity detection job is currently being developed using field sensors that can capture contextual data for static According to Pham and colleagues [45], Optitrackg. Optitrack cameras, environmental sensors, and embedded sensors in smartwatches can all be utilized to capture video and audio signals in conjunction with specialist wearables for physiological parameters [45]. Home gateways perform data preprocessing localization, while a private cloud stores information that can be accessed remotely. This is a fog-to-cloud architecture that works together cooperatively.

A number of authors, including Uddin [46] and Ram et al. [47], have written about fog designs. As demonstrated by Uddin [46], recurrent neural networks (RNN) and wearable sensors can be used to identify twelve different categories of human behaviors, while support vector machines (SVM) and random forest (RF) classifiers may be used to anticipate what people will do next, as demonstrated by Uddin [47]. Several recent ideas in the field of wearable sensor data analysis have begun to explore the application of edge machine learning techniques in this context. To solve the problem of finding irregularities in physiological measurements, [48] employed an edge-stream computing architecture. With the implementation of the HTM algorithm on a distributed network, only the edge nodes participate in computation during the inference process [49]. Queralta and colleagues [50] have developed an edge-based fall detection system that makes use of an LSTM recurrent neural network to detect a fall. EEG data from the research of [51] is used to examine how the Multi-Access Edge Computing concept and its application work in practice. Edge-side functions must be provided in order to meet application needs, and several traditional classifiers are compared for their accuracy. Azimi et al. [51] now describe ECG irregularities in a novel fashion. Using a variant of the IBM-developed MAPE-K model, the Hierarchical Computing Architecture for Healthcare (HiCH) is able to distribute computations across the three levels. The model is made up of four main parts: measure, analyze, and plan. A Monitor establishes a link between sensors and cloud machines, and a Plan executes the trained model. Analyze is responsible for heavy computational activities (model training). This method has been used to test both linear and deep learning algorithms.

8.3.2. Systems of Rehabilitation

Preventing infection and other difficulties with rehabilitation systems through the use of IoMT technology may improve post-operative health monitoring [52]. According to Mathur et al. [53], this data is transmitted to a fog station, where machine learning algorithms are used to make predictions regarding the health of a lower-limb amputee's residual leg. This is further supported by Villeneuve et al. [54], who use two low-power accelerometers mounted on the forearm to estimate simplified human limb motion [55]. A number of projects inspired by the MCC have looked into the fields of voice pathology and speech monitoring. Muhammad and colleagues [56] discuss speech pathology sensing devices that evaluate data from the device and wearable sensors and make use of powerful machine learning techniques in the cloud to attempt to learn machine categorization. For the treatment of Parkinson's disease patients, [57] and [27] use fog architecture to build speech surveillance systems that monitor and record their speech. In order to get acoustic properties, the data from a smart watch sensor is transferred to a fog node and classified in the cloud by a cloud classification service.

8.3.3. Skin Pathologies and Nutritional Evaluation

Because of the widespread use of mobile deep learning frameworks, which are designed for the purpose of doing DL interpretation directly on smartphones [58], a slew of exciting solutions in the field of smart health care are beginning to emerge. An approach to skin cancer diagnosis based on a previously trained CNN model that works on a Smartphone and performs the classification of skin lesions without the usage of a cloud computing system has been proposed by Dai et al. [59], and it is described in detail in the paper. An investigation into visual food identification was carried out with the goal of nutritional analysis as per a method proposed by Liu and colleagues [60].

8.3.4. Disease Control and Location-aware Solutions for Epidemics

As technology advances, the use of Internet-of-things devices in the identification and treatment of epidemic illnesses is becoming a more viable alternative. In these instances, intelligent data integration from multiple sensors, as well as real-time operation from diverse sensors, is all critical considerations. These systems are capable of reliably diagnosing virus infections at an early stage, allowing for timely treatment and a rapid return to normal function. Sood and Mahajan [61] describe a novel strategy to identify and prevent Chikungunya epidemics, which is described in detail. It is possible for a fog-based virus detection system to analyze the health symptoms of users as well as their surroundings and then send out alarm signals to alert them when they are in an area where they are at risk. The implementation of an MCC paradigm, as proposed by Sareen et al. [62], may be effective in both preventing and controlling Zika virus disease. The goal is to identify users who may be affected and display them on a Google map along with mosquito-dense areas and breeding sites in order to raise awareness. Fog layer: Processing and early analysis are always done in this layer. Cloud-based computing resources are used for storage, in-depth analysis, and remote access in every case, no matter what.

It has become necessary to develop rapid screening devices for the COVID-19 pandemic, which may be used to assess the presence of the primary indications of infection in contactless settings, and prototypes developed. According to Hegde et al. [63], a real-time DL algorithm could be used to recognize the forehead and lips using an infrared camera, whereas the properties can be used to detect cyanosis in the lips using a visible spectrum camera. An example of real-time DL algorithmic detection can be found in this system. In an IoMT framework, confidence is among the most important ways to share information. As explained by Al-Hamdi and Chen [64], an individual user's health loss risk can be estimated using sensors. Individual IoT devices provide data to a centralized cloud, which processes and analyses it. IoHT is rapidly being used in medical treatment, allowing for on-demand drug supply or rehabilitation. In this area, Masip-Bruin et al. [65] have investigated a breath assistance system for COPD that makes use of edge-to-cloud computing technologies (COPD). Smart portable oxygen concentrators (POCs) may be used by patients with COPD to modify and customize their oxygen dosages in real time based on their present environment and requirements according to their condition. Contextual information would be collected and processed on a regular basis, making sure that each patient's treatment is tailored to his or her unique habits.

8.4. Taxonomy of Smart Health

Smart healthcare taxonomy and parameters shown in Figure 8.4 below.

8.4.1. IoT Healthcare Services

The Internet of Things is expected to offer a wide range of healthcare support and services, each of which will include a number of healthcare possibilities. Healthcare and Internet of Things healthcare services, on the other hand, lack common criteria. Due to technical limitations, a service may not be able to be totally separated from a particular solution or service in some cases. Ambient Assisted Living (AAL): An AAL is defined as "services, ideas, and devices that enable the integration of technology with the social context to improve the overall quality of life." The Golden Rule inspires AAL's purpose to provide older people with the freedom to live in their homes in a helpful and safe manner. In addition to providing remote support in the event of a crisis, AAL administrations also provide self-governance services to their residents [66].

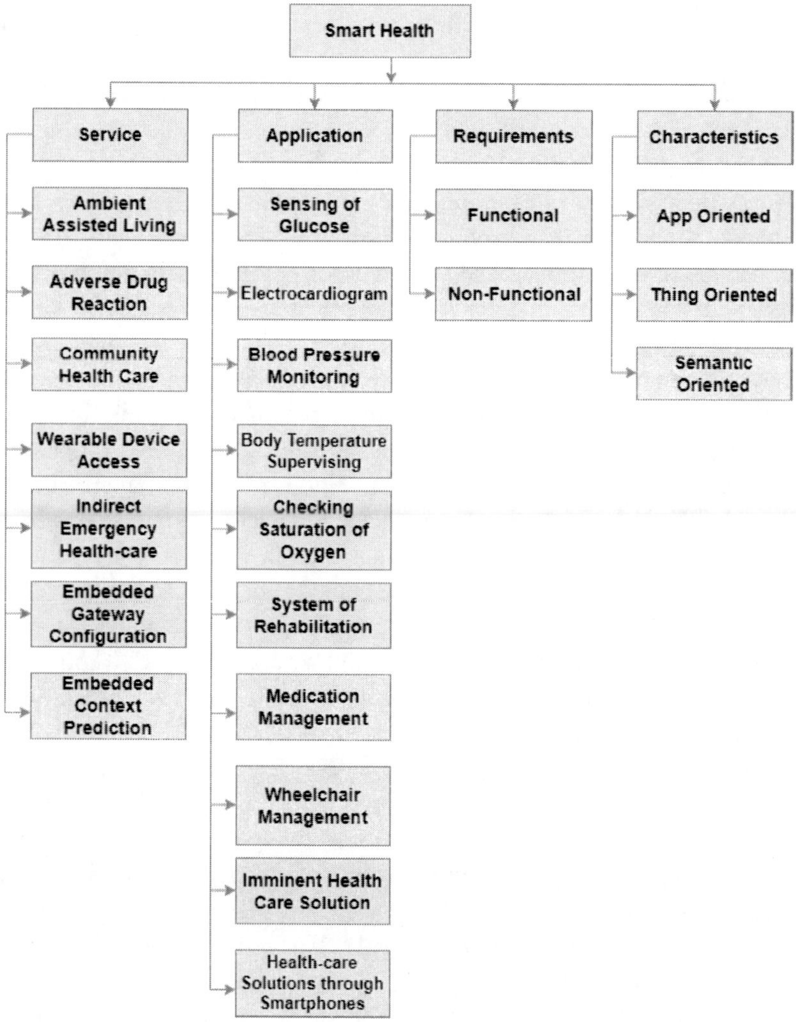

Figure 8.4. Smart healthcare taxonomy and parameters.

Adverse Drug Reaction (ADR): An ADR refers to a reaction that occurs after a patient takes a prescribed medicine. Adverse drug reactions are frequently caused by taking an extremely high dose or by taking a large number of medications at the same time. However, even though ADRs are meant to cover a wide range of illnesses and medications, it is recommended that some of the most common speciality disorders and their treatments be covered. Using barcode/NFC-authorized gadgets and other methods, the medicine can be detected on the patient's side. The data is processed in a way that ensures that it is correct in order to find medications that are right for the patient's allergy profile and electronic health history.

Community Health Care: Creating a local network of health care providers and facilities is the foundation of community health care (CHs). Internet of Things-based systems could be used in places outside of metropolitan areas, rural areas and residential neighborhoods. Several networks linked in this way could be considered excellent designs for networks... In order to meet the unique needs of a large group of individuals, these situations necessitate the employment of a specialist service known as community health care. In rural health care, the Internet of Things (IoT) has been found to be energy efficient and is a beneficial tool, [67] illustrating this idea. Cooperative networks need distinct authentication and authorization processes be integrated, hence this is suggested. [68] proposes the establishment of a network for community medications. There are many WBANs (Wireless BANs) that are utilized to create CH in this network. The 'Virtual Medical-Health-Care Center' has a lot in common with the network concept for community medicines. Wearable Device Access (WDA): A wide array of non-intrusive sensors can be employed for a number of medical applications in WSN-based medical health care services. The same devices can be used to provide the same services on the Internet of Things. Wearable gadgets are possible because of a number of IoT-friendly features. As a result, designers and analysts working on wearable device integrations confront a challenge in matching the demands of diverse sensors and components. There are WSN-based IoT applications detailed in [69]. Using this paradigm, medical health care apps can be developed on a wide range of mobile devices, including smartwatches and smartphones.

Indirect Emergency Health Care (IEH): The provision of medical services is often essential in these situations. A few instances of these events are incompatible climatic conditions, fire disasters, and in-flight incidents. Is it possible to make provisions for things like data access and notification of changes, as well as record keeping and post-accident activities? That's what the International Emergency Response Team says. Embedded Gateway Configuration (EGC): EGC is a medical composition facility in charge of connecting network nodes, inter-networks, and other necessary systems. However, it all depends on the specific purpose of the communicated gateway, a number of common integration elements may be required, which may or may not be applicable. Because it is a part of the universal healthcare system, an EGC facility is examined in [70] because it allows for computerized and intelligent monitoring. Embedded Context Prediction (ECP): Third-party developers that want to create context-aware (CA) medical healthcare apps need a service known as the ECP service. In terms of universal health coverage, a comparable system may be found in [71]. In [72], a number of issues in the California healthcare system are examined. Remote health monitoring using IoT-based context prediction has similar issues to the aforementioned system's uses.

8.4.2. Healthcare Applications

As a result of the development of smart healthcare services, applications are created that customers and patients can correctly employ. Sensing of Glucose: When a person's blood glucose levels are too high, it's considered a diabetic infection. As a result of monitoring blood glucose, a person can plan their diet, exercise, and medication schedules accordingly. [73] outlines a new m-IoT design approach for measuring glucose levels in real-time. Electrocardiogram (ECG) Supervision: An ECG includes the estimation of the straight-forward pulse and the declaration of vital rhythm, as well as the detection of difficult arrhythmias and extended QT intervals. Blood Pressure Monitoring: Using sensors like a digital pressure and pulsating sensor, blood pressure monitors pick up on pulsation and pressure signals and digitally show the results. Data from a blood pressure monitor can be transmitted via an IoT network by the device shown in [74]. The gadget consists of a mechanical component for measuring blood pressure and a communication module. An IoT terminal for continuous blood pressure monitoring is described [75].

Body Temperature Monitoring: It is an essential component of smart healthcare. The importance of keeping a constant body temperature cannot be overstated. According to [76], mill trail data is utilized to verify that an m-IoT system implanted in TelosB monitors the body temperature and is functioning as planned. Examining Oxygen Saturation: In a non-invasive manner, heartbeat oximetry can be used to monitor blood oxygen saturation. The integration of heartbeat oximetry and the Internet of Things is beneficial for changing health care software. In a CoAP-based smart healthcare review, IoT-based heartbeat oximetry is discussed [77]. Yang et al. [78] OX2 wrist oximeter measures heart rate using blood oxygen concentration. This wearable device uses sensors that use Bluetooth health profiles when it is connected to the Monere platform. System of Rehabilitation: Drugs and recuperation can help people with physical weakness or disability improve and restore their usefulness and personal enjoyment. Internet of Things (IoT) can help rehabilitation by storing medical experts' data. Informed medical treatment in [79], an ontology-based automation technique for IoT rehabilitation systems is described. Connecting each significant advantage to the IoT is proved to be a successful step in providing constant data transfer. Medication Management: Drugs and rehabilitation can assist people with physical weakness or disability in improving and restoring their usefulness and personal enjoyment. of Things (IoT) can help rehabilitation by storing medical experts' data. Informed medical treatment in [79], an ontology-based automation technique for IoT rehabilitation systems is described. Connecting each significant advantage to the IoT has proved to be a successful phase in allow constant data transfer. Wheelchair Management: A number of scientific endeavours have been made to produce intelligent wheelchairs that are constructed using a thorough mechanism for people who are physically handicapped. The Internet of Things has the potential to help with these kinds of issues.

8.4.3. Smart Healthcare Requirements

As shown in Figure 8.5, the functional and non-functional needs of smart health care can be comprehensively organized. Technical specs are concerned with the design's special needs. If, for example, a temperature monitoring system is used to monitor a certain application's temperature, the thermometer/operating thermistor's range, data gathering method, and frequency of operation may differ. As a result, functional requirements are specific to the different segments used in the smart healthcare system, depending on their intended use. Non-functional specifications, on the other hand, can be vague. This criterion signifies the presence of features that can be used to address problems in the healthcare system. Ethics and performance standards are two broad categories into which non-functional necessities of health care can be grouped. There are a lot of problems with designing an intelligent health care system as a whole, so performance requirements are further broken down into hardware and software requirements. As a result, the primary focus of design and intelligent health care is to ensure speedy access to health care. Additional requirements for cutting-edge applications necessitate ambient intelligence to enhance the facility's character.

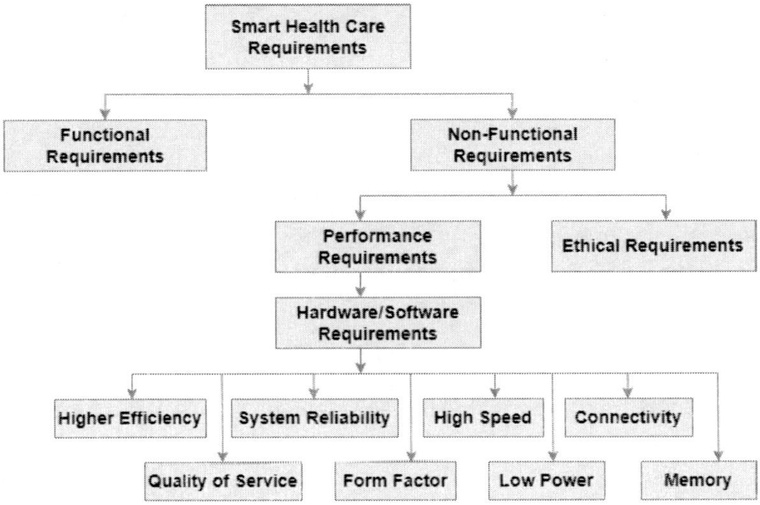

Figure 8.5. Requirements for smart healthcare.

In the subject of smart healthcare, researchers and projects come from a wide range of perspectives, depending on the desired objective. The sensors, automation systems, data storage components, and system components of an intelligent health care technique can be identified. When a sensor and an organic element work together to detect events, it is referred to as a sensor. Depending on the monitoring system, sensors or actuators may be used that are not the same. In a smart health care system, sensors like EMG, blood pressure, ECG, and temperature sensors are all common, as are SpO2, accelerometers, orientation sensors, and sensors that track movement. PDAs, smartphones, and tablets are the simplest computers. Super PCs and servers are the most complex and advanced. As the most critical component of the systems, storage has an important role in intelligent health care. The innovative health-care network's information repository components ensure a wider range, starting with implanted memory on detection devices and gigantic servers used to handle large information analyses.

8.4.4. Characteristics of Smart Healthcare

Figure 8.6 depicts the most significant needs for a successful implementation of the smart health care system. Things-oriented, App-oriented, and Semantics-oriented are the three basic categories of requirements. It is the only responsibility of App-oriented architectures to ensure the integrity of data flows between applications in smartphones and sensors by ensuring the construction of a customized network. Thing-oriented architectural designs are responsible for quick oversight, adaptability in use, responsiveness at the highest level, power efficiency, and the ability to turn on intelligent procedures. Users should be able to employ Semantic-oriented systems to improve their user experience, grow detectable specimens based on previously gathered data, and have extraordinary computational capabilities.

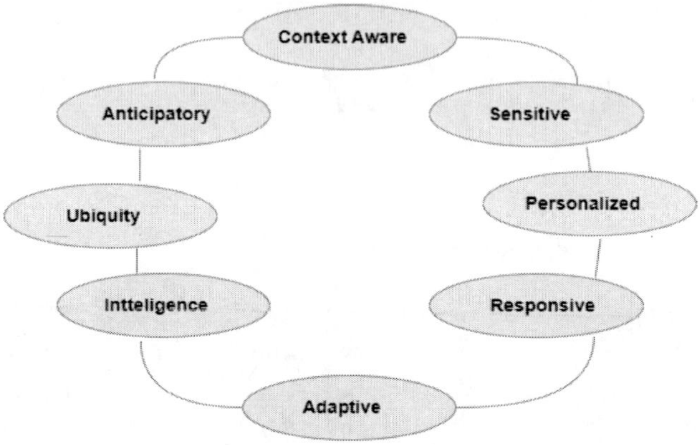

Figure 8.6. Characteristics of smart health care.

Conclusion

Health monitoring systems for smart healthcare provide a secure, effective, and simply deployable health monitoring system that can assure high-quality healthcare services at a fraction of the price presently borne by hospitals or assisted-living facilities. The state-of-the-art wearable gadgets and smartphones for basic indicators monitoring, as well as machine learning for chronic disease detection, were covered in detail in this review. These frameworks for software integration, which are extremely important in the development of smart healthcare, are summarized in this study and discussed in detail. Several systems have been examined in detail, both for their advantages and for their drawbacks. In addition, we reviewed the major issues of recently developed smart healthcare frameworks, which are the primary impediments to the development of prototypes to assist the disabled. For the purpose of further improving the existing healthcare system, some prospective future research directions are suggested for consideration. Although technology will never be able to completely replace the medical system, it will be able to minimize the strain on medical specialists by introducing some unique structures. Development of such assistive systems might be achievable if medical specialists and researchers collaborated on a platform to make the systems available to the public.

References

[1] Nasr, Mahmoud, Md Milon Islam, Shady Shehata, Fakhri Karray, and Yuri Quintana. "Smart healthcare in the age of AI: recent advances, challenges, and future prospects." *IEEE Access* (2021).

[2] Calvaresi, Davide, Daniel Cesarini, Paolo Sernani, Mauro Marinoni, Aldo Franco Dragoni, and Arnon Sturm. "Exploring the ambient assisted living domain: a systematic review." *Journal of Ambient Intelligence and Humanized Computing* 8, no. 2 (2017): 239-257.

[3] Charulatha, A. R., and R. Sujatha. "Smart healthcare use cases and applications." In *Internet of Things Use Cases for the Healthcare Industry,* pp. 185-203. Springer, Cham, 2020.

[4] Patton, Mike. "US health care costs rise faster than inflation." Retrieved from *Forbes:* https://scholar. google. com/scholar (2015).

[5] Baker, Stephanie B., Wei Xiang, and Ian Atkinson. "Internet of things for smart healthcare: Technologies, challenges, and opportunities." *IEEE Access* 5 (2017): 26521-26544.

[6] Rghioui, Amine, and Abdelmajid Oumnad. "Challenges and Opportunities of Internet of Things in Healthcare." *International Journal of Electrical & Computer Engineering* (2088-8708) 8, no. 5 (2018).

[7] Zhu, Hongxu, Chung Kit Wu, Cheon Hoi Koo, Yee Ting Tsang, Yucheng Liu, Hao Ran Chi, and Kim-Fung Tsang. "Smart healthcare in the era of internet-of-things." *IEEE Consumer Electronics Magazine* 8, no. 5 (2019): 26-30.

[8] Dash, Sabyasachi, Sushil Kumar Shakyawar, Mohit Sharma, and Sandeep Kaushik. "Big data in healthcare: management, analysis and future prospects." *Journal of Big Data* 6, no. 1 (2019): 1-25.

[9] Bahri, Safa, Nesrine Zoghlami, Mourad Abed, and João Manuel RS Tavares. "Big data for healthcare: a survey." *IEEE access* 7 (2018): 7397-7408.

[10] Ali, Omar, Anup Shrestha, Jeffrey Soar, and Samuel Fosso Wamba. "Cloud computing-enabled healthcare opportunities, issues, and applications: A systematic review." *International Journal of Information Management* 43 (2018): 146-158.

[11] Gao, Fangjian, and Ali Sunyaev. "Context matters: A review of the determinant factors in the decision to adopt cloud computing in healthcare." *International Journal of Information Management* 48 (2019): 120-138.

[12] Wood, Ethan, Dean Mohamedally, Neil J. Sebire, and Sheena Visram. "44 Internet of healthcare things (IoHT) handheld device for secure patient data retrieval." *Digital Poster Presentations* (2020): A15-A15.

[13] Kaur, Harleen, Mohd Atif, and Ritu Chauhan. "An internet of healthcare things (IoHT)-based healthcare monitoring system." In *Advances in intelligent computing and communication,* pp. 475-482. Springer, Singapore, 2020.

[14] Joyia, Gulraiz J., Rao M. Liaqat, Aftab Farooq, and Saad Rehman. "Internet of medical things (IoMT): Applications, benefits and future challenges in healthcare domain." *J. Commun.* 12, no. 4 (2017): 240-247.

[15] Parvathy, Velmurugan Subbiah, Sivakumar Pothiraj, and Jenyfal Sampson. "Automated internet of medical things (iomt) based healthcare monitoring system." In *Cognitive Internet of Medical Things for Smart Healthcare,* pp. 117-128. Springer, Cham, 2021.

[16] Majumder, Sumit, Tapas Mondal, and M. Jamal Deen. "Wearable sensors for remote health monitoring." *Sensors* 17, no. 1 (2017): 130.

[17] Dias, Duarte, and João Paulo Silva Cunha. "Wearable health devices—vital sign monitoring, systems and technologies." *Sensors* 18, no. 8 (2018): 2414.

[18] Islam, Md, Saifuddin Mahmud, L. J. Muhammad, Sheikh Nooruddin, and Safial Islam Ayon. "Wearable technology to assist the patients infected with novel coronavirus (COVID-19)." *SN computer science* 1, no. 6 (2020): 1-9.

[19] Dian, F. John, Reza Vahidnia, and Alireza Rahmati. "Wearables and the Internet of Things (IoT), applications, opportunities, and challenges: A Survey." *IEEE Access* 8 (2020): 69200-69211.

[20] Islam, Md, and Ashikur Rahaman. "Development of smart healthcare monitoring system in IoT environment." *SN computer science* 1, no. 3 (2020): 1-11.

[21] Wan, Jie, Munassar AAH Al-awlaqi, MingSong Li, Michael O'Grady, Xiang Gu, Jin Wang, and Ning Cao. "Wearable IoT enabled real-time health monitoring system." *EURASIP Journal on Wireless Communications and Networking 2018,* no. 1 (2018): 1-10.

[22] Yuri Quintana, Darren Fahy, Bradley Crotty, Ruchira Jain, Eli Kaldany, Maxwel Gorenberg, Lewis Lipsitz, Diane Engorn, Jorge Rodriguez, Alex Orfanos, Adarsha Bajracharya, Juan Henao, May Adra, David Skerry, Warner V. Slack and Charles Safran. "Infosage: Supporting elders and families through online family networks." In *AMIA Annual Symposium Proceedings,* vol. 2018, p. 932. American Medical Informatics Association, 2018.

[23] Majumder, Sumit, and M. Jamal Deen. "Smartphone sensors for health monitoring and diagnosis." *Sensors* 19, no. 9 (2019): 2164.

[24] Zhang, Gaobo, Zhen Mei, Yuan Zhang, Xuesheng Ma, Benny Lo, Dongyi Chen, and Yuanting Zhang. "A noninvasive blood glucose monitoring system based on smartphone PPG signal processing and machine learning." *IEEE Transactions on Industrial Informatics* 16, no. 11 (2020): 7209-7218.

[25] Tabei, Fatemehsadat, Jon Michael Gresham, Behnam Askarian, Kwanghee Jung, and Jo Woon Chong. "Cuff-less blood pressure monitoring system using smartphones." *IEEE Access* 8 (2020): 11534-11545.

[26] Dubey, Harishchandra, Jing Yang, Nick Constant, Amir Mohammad Amiri, Qing Yang, and Kunal Makodiya. "Fog data: Enhancing telehealth big data through fog computing." In *Proceedings of the ASE bigdata & social informatics* 2015, pp. 1-6. 2015.

[27] Le, Dac-Nhuong, Velmurugan Subbiah Parvathy, Deepak Gupta, Ashish Khanna, Joel JPC Rodrigues, and K. Shankar. "IoT enabled depthwise separable convolution neural network with deep support vector machine for COVID-19 diagnosis and classification." *International Journal of Machine Learning and Cybernetics* 12, no. 11 (2021): 3235-3248.

[28] Karmore, Swapnili, Rushikesh Bodhe, Fadi Al-Turjman, R. Lakshmana Kumar, and Sofia Pillai. "IoT based humanoid software for identification and diagnosis of Covid-19 suspects." *IEEE Sensors Journal* (2020).

[29] Cacovean, Dan, Irina Ioana, and Gabriela Nitulescu. "IoT system in diagnosis of Covid-19 patients." *Informatica Economica* 24, no. 2 (2020): 75-89.

[30] Ali, Farman, Shaker El-Sappagh, SM Riazul Islam, Daehan Kwak, Amjad Ali, Muhammad Imran, and Kyung-Sup Kwak. "A smart healthcare monitoring system for heart disease prediction based on ensemble deep learning and feature fusion." *Information Fusion* 63 (2020): 208-222.

[31] Deperlioglu, Omer, Utku Kose, Deepak Gupta, Ashish Khanna, and Arun Kumar Sangaiah. "Diagnosis of heart diseases by a secure internet of health things system based on autoencoder deep neural network." *Computer Communications* 162 (2020): 31-50.

[32] Khan, Mohammad Ayoub, and Fahad Algarni. "A healthcare monitoring system for the diagnosis of heart disease in the IoMT cloud environment using MSSO-ANFIS." *IEEE Access* 8 (2020): 122259-122269.

[33] Rghioui, Amine, Assia Naja, Jaime Lloret Mauri, and Abedlmajid Oumnad. "An IOT based diabetic patient monitoring system using machine learning and node MCU." In *Journal of Physics: Conference Series*, vol. 1743, no. 1, p. 012035. IOP Publishing, 2021.

[34] Punitha Ponmalar, P., and C. R. Vijayalakshmi. "Aggregation in IoT for Prediction of Diabetics with Machine Learning Techniques." In *International conference on Computer Networks, Big data and IoT,* pp. 789-798. Springer, Cham, 2019.

[35] Komai, Kiyoaki, Manato Fujimoto, Yutaka Arakawa, Hirohiko Suwa, Yukitoshi Kashimoto, and Keiichi Yasumoto. "Beacon-based multi-person activity monitoring system for day care center." In *2016 IEEE International Conference on Pervasive Computing and Communication Workshops* (PerCom Workshops), pp. 1-6. IEEE, 2016.

[36] Marques, Gonçalo, Ivan Miguel Pires, Nuno Miranda, and Rui Pitarma. "Air quality monitoring using assistive robots for ambient assisted living and enhanced living environments through internet of things." *Electronics* 8, no. 12 (2019): 1375.

[37] Syed, Liyakathunisa, Saima Jabeen, S. Manimala, and Abdullah Alsaeedi. "Smart healthcare framework for ambient assisted living using IoMT and big data analytics techniques." *Future Generation Computer Systems* 101 (2019): 136-151.

[38] Stavrotheodoros, Stefanos, Nikolaos Kaklanis, and Dimitrios Tzovaras. "A personalized cloud-based platform for AAL support to cognitively impaired elderly

people." In *International Conference on Biomedical and Health Informatics,* pp. 87-91. Springer, Singapore, 2017.

[39] Bedaf, Sandra, Patrizia Marti, Farshid Amirabdollahian, and Luc de Witte. "A multi-perspective evaluation of a service robot for seniors: the voice of different stakeholders." *Disability and Rehabilitation: Assistive Technology* 13, no. 6 (2018): 592-599.

[40] Lee, Sukhan, and Ahmed M. Naguib. "Toward a sociable and dependable elderly care robot: design, implementation and user study." *Journal of Intelligent & Robotic Systems* 98, no. 1 (2020): 5-17.

[41] Portugal, David, Luís Santos, Paulo Alvito, Jorge Dias, George Samaras, and Eleni Christodoulou. "SocialRobot: An interactive mobile robot for elderly home care." In *2015 IEEE/SICE International Symposium on System Integration (SII),* pp. 811-816. IEEE, 2015.

[42] Magaña-Espinoza, Pedro, Raúl Aquino-Santos, Néstor Cárdenas-Benítez, José Aguilar-Velasco, César Buenrostro-Segura, Arthur Edwards-Block, and Aldo Medina-Cass. "WiSPH: A wireless sensor network-based home care monitoring system." *Sensors* 14, no. 4 (2014): 7096-7119.

[43] Alwan, Omar S., and K. Prahald Rao. "Dedicated real-time monitoring system for health care using ZigBee." *Healthcare Technology Letters* 4, no.4 (2017): 142-144.

[44] Satija, Udit, Barathram Ramkumar, and M. Sabarimalai Manikandan. "Real-time signal quality-aware ECG telemetry system for IoT-based health care monitoring." *IEEE Internet of Things Journal* 4, no. 3 (2017): 815-823.

[45] Pham, Minh, Yehenew Mengistu, Ha Do, and Weihua Sheng. "Delivering home healthcare through a cloud-based smart home environment (CoSHE)." *Future Generation Computer Systems* 81 (2018): 129-140.

[46] Uddin, Md Zia. "A wearable sensor-based activity prediction system to facilitate edge computing in smart healthcare system." *Journal of Parallel and Distributed Computing* 123 (2019): 46-53.

[47] Ram, Sigdel Shree, Bernady Apduhan, and Norio Shiratori. "A machine learning framework for edge computing to improve prediction accuracy in mobile health monitoring." In *International Conference on Computational Science and Its Applications,* pp. 417-431. Springer, Cham, 2019.

[48] Greco, Luca, Pierluigi Ritrovato, and Fatos Xhafa. "An edge-stream computing infrastructure for real-time analysis of wearable sensors data." *Future Generation Computer Systems* 93 (2019): 515-528.

[49] Abdellatif, Alaa Awad, Amr Mohamed, Carla Fabiana Chiasserini, Mounira Tlili, and Aiman Erbad. "Edge computing for smart health: Context-aware approaches, opportunities, and challenges." *IEEE Network* 33, no. 3 (2019): 196-203.

[50] Queralta, J. Pena, Tuan Nguyen Gia, Hannu Tenhunen, and Tomi Westerlund. "Edge-AI in LoRa-based health monitoring: Fall detection system with fog computing and LSTM recurrent neural networks." In *2019 42nd international conference on telecommunications and signal processing* (TSP), pp. 601-604. IEEE, 2019.

[51] Azimi, Iman, Janne Takalo-Mattila, Arman Anzanpour, Amir M. Rahmani, Juha-Pekka Soininen, and Pasi Liljeberg. "Empowering healthcare IoT systems with

hierarchical edge-based deep learning." In *Proceedings of the 2018 IEEE/ACM International Conference on Connected Health: Applications, Systems and Engineering Technologies,* pp. 63-68. 2018.

[52] Akmandor, Ayten Ozge, and Niraj K. Jha. "Smart health care: An edge-side computing perspective." *IEEE Consumer Electronics Magazine* 7, no. 1 (2017): 29-37.

[53] Mathur, Neha, Greig Paul, James Irvine, Mohamed Abuhelala, Arjan Buis, and Ivan Glesk. "A practical design and implementation of a low cost platform for remote monitoring of lower limb health of amputees in the developing world." *IEEE Access* 4 (2016): 7440-7451.

[54] Villeneuve, Emma, William Harwin, William Holderbaum, Balazs Janko, and R. Simon Sherratt. "Reconstruction of angular kinematics from wrist-worn inertial sensor data for smart home healthcare." *IEEE Access* 5 (2017): 2351-2363.

[55] Muhammad, Ghulam, SK Md Mizanur Rahman, Abdulhameed Alelaiwi, and Atif Alamri. "Smart health solution integrating IoT and cloud: A case study of voice pathology monitoring." *IEEE Communications Magazine* 55, no. 1 (2017): 69-73.

[56] Muhammad, Ghulam, Mohammed F. Alhamid, Mansour Alsulaiman, and Brij Gupta. "Edge computing with cloud for voice disorder assessment and treatment." *IEEE Communications Magazine* 56, no. 4 (2018): 60-65.

[57] Villarrubia, Gabriel, Javier Bajo, Juan F. De Paz, and Juan M. Corchado. "Monitoring and detection platform to prevent anomalous situations in home care." *Sensors* 14, no. 6 (2014): 9900-9921.

[58] Monteiro, Admir, Harishchandra Dubey, Leslie Mahler, Qing Yang, and Kunal Mankodiya. "Fit: A fog computing device for speech tele-treatments." In *2016 IEEE international conference on smart computing (SMARTCOMP),* pp. 1-3. IEEE, 2016.

[59] Dai, Xiangfeng, Irena Spasić, Bradley Meyer, Samuel Chapman, and Frederic Andres. "Machine learning on mobile: An on-device inference app for skin cancer detection." In *2019 Fourth International Conference on Fog and Mobile Edge Computing (FMEC),* pp. 301-305. IEEE, 2019.

[60] Liu, Chang, Yu Cao, Yan Luo, Guanling Chen, Vinod Vokkarane, Ma Yunsheng, Songqing Chen, and Peng Hou. "A new deep learning-based food recognition system for dietary assessment on an edge computing service infrastructure." *IEEE Transactions on Services Computing* 11, no. 2 (2017): 249-261.

[61] Sood, Sandeep K., and Isha Mahajan. "A fog-based healthcare framework for chikungunya." *IEEE Internet of Things Journal* 5, no. 2 (2017): 794-801.

[62] Sareen, Sanjay, Sunil Kumar Gupta, and Sandeep K. Sood. "An intelligent and secure system for predicting and preventing Zika virus outbreak using Fog computing." *Enterprise Information Systems* 11, no. 9 (2017): 1436-1456.

[63] Hegde, Chaitra, Zifan Jiang, Pradyumna Byappanahalli Suresha, Jacob Zelko, Salman Seyedi, Monique A. Smith, David W. Wright, Rishikesan Kamaleswaran, Matt A. Reyna, and Gari D. Clifford. "Autotriage-an open source edge computing raspberry pi-based clinical screening system." *medrxiv* (2020).

[64] Al-Hamadi, Hamid, and Ray Chen. "Trust-based decision making for health IoT systems." *IEEE Internet of Things Journal* 4, no. 5 (2017): 1408-1419.

[65] Masip-Bruin, Xavier, Eva Marín-Tordera, Albert Alonso, and Jordi Garcia. "Fog-to-cloud Computing (F2C): The key technology enabler for dependable e-health services deployment." In *2016 Mediterranean ad hoc networking workshop (Med-Hoc-Net),* pp. 1-5. IEEE, 2016.

[66] Mehmood, Yasir, Farhan Ahmad, Ibrar Yaqoob, Asma Adnane, Muhammad Imran, and Sghaier Guizani. "Internet-of-things-based smart cities: Recent advances and challenges." *IEEE Communications Magazine* 55, no. 9 (2017): 16-24.

[67] Islam, SM Riazul, Daehan Kwak, MD Humaun Kabir, Mahmud Hossain, and Kyung-Sup Kwak. "The internet of things for health care: a comprehensive survey." *IEEE Access* 3 (2015): 678-708.

[68] Rohokale, Vandana Milind, Neeli Rashmi Prasad, and Ramjee Prasad. "A cooperative Internet of Things (IoT) for rural healthcare monitoring and control." In *2011 2nd international conference on wireless communication, vehicular technology, information theory and aerospace & electronic systems technology (Wireless VITAE)*, pp. 1-6. IEEE, 2011.

[69] You, Lei, Chungui Liu, and Sen Tong. "Community medical network (CMN): Architecture and implementation." In *2011 Global Mobile Congress,* pp. 1-6. IEEE, 2011.

[70] Castillejo, Pedro, Jose-Fernan Martinez, Jesus Rodriguez-Molina, and Alexandra Cuerva. "Integration of wearable devices in a wireless sensor network for an E-health application." *IEEE Wireless Communications* 20, no. 4 (2013): 38-49.

[71] Rasid, Mohd Fadlee A., Wan Mardiana Wan Musa, Nurul Ashikin Abdul Kadir, Anas M. Noor, Farid Touati, Waiser Mehmood, Lazhar Khriji, Asma Al-Busaidi, and A. Ben Mnaouer. "Embedded gateway services for Internet of Things applications in ubiquitous healthcare." In *2014 2nd International Conference on Information and Communication Technology (ICoICT),* pp. 145-148. IEEE, 2014.

[72] De Brouwer, Mathias, Femke Ongenae, Pieter Bonte, and Filip De Turck. "Towards a cascading reasoning framework to support responsive ambient-intelligent healthcare interventions." *Sensors* 18, no. 10 (2018): 3514.

[73] Curran, Kevin, Gary Mansell, and Jack Curran. "An IoT Framework for Detecting Movement Within Indoor Environments." In *International Conference on Machine Learning for Networking,* pp. 333-340. Springer, Cham, 2018.

[74] Mi, Zhangpeng, and Gengyu Wei. "A CoAP-Based Smartphone Proxy for Healthcare with IoT Technologies." In *2018 IEEE 9th International Conference on Software Engineering and Service Science (ICSESS),* pp. 271-278. IEEE, 2018.

[75] Tabish, Rohan, Abdulaziz M. Ghaleb, Rima Hussein, Farid Touati, Adel Ben Mnaouer, Lazhar Khriji, and Mohd Fadlee A. Rasid. "A 3G/WiFi-enabled 6LoWPAN-based U-healthcare system for ubiquitous real-time monitoring and data logging." In *2nd Middle East Conference on Biomedical Engineering,* pp. 277-280. IEEE, 2014.

[76] Fan, Yuan Jie, Yue Hong Yin, Li Da Xu, Yan Zeng, and Fan Wu. "IoT-based smart rehabilitation system." *IEEE transactions on industrial informatics* 10, no. 2 (2014): 1568-1577.

[77] Pang, Zhibo, Junzhe Tian, and Qiang Chen. "Intelligent packaging and intelligent medicine box for medication management towards the Internet-of-Things." In *16th*

international conference on advanced communication technology, pp. 352-360. IEEE, 2014.

[78] Yang, Lin, Yanhong Ge, Wenfeng Li, Wenbi Rao, and Weiming Shen. "A home mobile healthcare system for wheelchair users." In P*roceedings of the 2014 IEEE 18th international conference on computer supported cooperative work in design (CSCWD),* pp. 609-614. IEEE, 2014.

[79] Papavasiliou, Pavlos, Tammy Fisher, Joseph Kuhn, John Nemunaitis, and Jeffrey Lamont. "Circulating tumor cells in patients undergoing surgery for hepatic metastases from colorectal cancer." In *Baylor University Medical Center Proceedings,* vol. 23, no. 1, pp. 11-14. Taylor & Francis, 2010.

Chapter 9

IoT-Based E-Health Monitoring System for Pre-Schoolers

Sumitra Samal* **and Tirna Mitra**
Computer Science & Engineering,
Shri Shankaracharya Institute of Professional Management and Technology,
Raipur (C.G.), India

Abstract

IoT (Internet of Things) technology has spread its wings in the medical field to save many lives. Through this paper, we are going to describe the details of the innovative device which will monitor the hydration level and oxygen saturation of the child. This device can detect whether the child is dehydrated or suffering from any disease related to lack of oxygen in their body which they fail to communicate to their parents. Which leads to the death of children under the age of five (the number of deaths globally reaches 5 million per year). We have developed a product using a medicated pacifier where the respective hydration and oxygen saturation levels are calculated, using sensors called DHT11 and MAX30100 sensors. These sensors are connected to the Wi-Fi integrated circuit controller board. The Wi-Fi module, that is the ESP8266, is connected to the sensors through which the data would be transferred wirelessly. The visualization of data would be done on the Blynk mobile application. The intersection is between the technological aspect and that of the healthcare sector is of the latest trend. Having stated that, the same is not applied in today's world as effectively as it should have due to the lack of infrastructure, manufacturing capacity and the help of political influencers. The segment of the Internet of Things is predicted to outdo

* Corresponding Author's Email: samal.sumitra07@gmail.com.

In: Applications of Artificial Intelligence in the Healthcare Sector
Editors: Jyoti Prakash Patra and Yogesh Kumar Rathore
ISBN: 979-8-88697-502-4

the current scenario of the medical sector associated with technology. IoT is expected to enhance e-health all over India, it would simplify and perform the data abstraction in such a way that these technologies would reach every corner of the Indian subcontinent, making it easy for the health caretakers to reach the mass and provide the required treatment, thereby ensuring a much better health sector across India.

Keywords: IoT, DHT11, WIFI module, Max30100 sensor, ESP8266, Blynk app

9.1. Introduction

In the recent past, the present, and in the future, wireless technology had immensely spread its wings, in almost all the sectors possible. Unfortunately, we tend to observe a steady increasing population and also the high rise of chronic unhealthiness that is exacting for a contemporary high technologically equipped tending system and the demand for resources from hospital beds to doctors and nurses is extraordinarily high. The Healthcare industry [1], in particular, has gone wireless extending to the fact that robots have now taken charge of complex surgery. Recently one of the main technologies that are at the top of the technological field is the Internet of Things. IoT has a major impact on the industrial area which concerns automation and control. The Biomedical Industry has a great trend in the present times to provide better health care facilities. Not only in hospitals but also one can enjoy the benefits provided by IoT on a personal level. The Internet of Things gives a growing era to reap the subsequent degree of fitness services. Hence, having a smart system that monitors several conditions that consume power is thereby used to observe an efficient result. Concerning the above-mentioned smart system, this paper is being reviewed. It is been so observed that children below the age of 5 years die due to dehydration and problems related to asphyxia. The death numbers are observed to be touching five million each year globally (data collected from a team named Rehydration Project). Since children are unable to convey their problems or they are not old enough to understand what exactly the problem is with their body, it becomes very difficult to provide proper medication at a proper time especially when the parents are working. With the help of this modern approach [2], time consumption can be highly reduced. The pacifier is attached with a hydration sensor as well as a Spo2 tracking sensor inbuilt within the holding loop of the pacifier which would be in the form of the ring that the child would wear all the time, which would thereby gather the information from the body and transfer to the corresponding mobile application. If the value falls or rises below or above the critical values, an alert would be shown. At present, the usage of high technology, associated with wireless appliances has been increasing at a greater pace in almost all sectors of society. In these recent years, IoT has evolved the most in the industrial area, especially in automation and control. Aerial access networks are recognized as a key enabler of assorted Internet-of-Things (IoT) services and applications in future sixth-generation (6G) wireless systems. The internet of Things (IoT) has been widely known as a potential goal to lighten the tensions in medical care frameworks and has consequently been the principal focal point of a great deal of late investigation. Biomedicals is one of the recent higher technology evolving which aims to provide better health care to every individual. Not only in hospitals but also in the personal health care department, the Internet of Things has proven its benefits. So, having a personal smart system, which monitors various parameters and guides the user as to what step is to be taken next to attain the best health. The commitment of IoT in the medical region is vital to us and can't be disregarded.

9.2. Literature Survey

The Internet of Things is an assortment of actual gadgets which could incorporate more modest modules, vehicles, mechanized home machines, and different things which are inserted with programming, sensors, batteries, actuators, and networks (like actual associations or Wi-Fi associations) which empowers the joined pieces of the gadget to interface and trade information and data. An extensive amount of this examination shows up in the perception of patients with explicit circumstances values polygenic sickness or Parkinson's illness [3]. extra exploration hopes to fill explicit needs, for example, helping restoration through steady checking of a patient's advancement. Crisis consideration has also been known as an open door by associated works anyway has not regardless been investigated broadly. a few related research works have previously been exhausted in unambiguous regions any place advancements are utilized including IoT [4]. A top to bottom overview is yielded, with center put around financially available arrangements, potential applications, and remaining issues. every subject is investigated independently, as opposed to as a portion of a whole framework. In data mining, stockpiling, and examination are thought of, with very little notice of coordination of these into a framework. sensor assortments are analyzed in, with some emphasis put on correspondences. Nonetheless, drawing a whole picture of the framework from this paper is hard. At long last, detecting and enormous data, the executives are thought of, with little respect for the organization that will uphold interchanges.

The NodeMCU (Node Microcontroller Unit) is open-source programming and equipment that is a firmware improvement climate for which a comparative climate, which is the open-source prototyping board is constructed. It is encircled by a cheap System-on-a-Chip (SoC) called the ESP8266. The NodeMCU ESP8266 advancement board accompanies the ESP-12E. This expressed chip can uphold RTOS and its activity is at 80MHz to 160 MHz which has a customizable clock recurrence. The NodeMCU has just about 128 KB RAM and 4MB of Flash memory for the capacity of information and projects which are scorched in it. The ESP8266 was planned and produced by Espressif Systems. It has a high handling power alongside an in-constructed Wi-Fi/Bluetooth network choice and Deep Sleep Operating elements which makes it ideal for creating IoT projects. NodeMCU can achieve the power required to run the project from a Micro USB jack and a VIN pin (External Supply Pin). Features like UART, SPI, and I2C interface are also supported by this. The programming that is to be done in the NodeMCU Development Board can be easily done with the help of the development environment named Arduino IDE as it is easy to implement. The code which is to be implemented in the NodeMCU with the help of the software as stated by Arduino IDE does not take much time, which is approximately 5 to 10 minutes. The main things which are required are the Arduino IDE, the main NodeMCU board and a USB cable. If one is comfortable with the programming syntax and methodology of Node.js then it is similar to that of programming the NodeMCU programming model. This model can be stated as an asynchronous and also event-driven model. The callback function is available for many functions. There are many packaging styles available in the NodeMCU. The base ESP8266 core is the basic commonality for all the designs. The standard 30-pin layout is being maintained by the designs which are based on architecture. One of the main important considerations that are to be aware of is that certain designs have usage of a rather common and narrow (0.9”) footprint whereas the others have usage of a comparatively wide (1.1”) footprint. (One of the most common models of the programmable model, NodeMCU are Amica (which is based on the standard narrow pin-spacing) and LoLin which has the wider pin spacing along with a larger board. Since the base ESP8266 is an open-source design, this factor enables the market to create newer, more efficient and varied models to be developed continuously. Despite having all the benefits, it has an issue which is that the ESP8266 is hard to access and it is hard to use. Even for a simple task, for example, such as powering the setup or sending a basic notification to the model, one has to solder wires, with a proper connection with analog voltage associated with its respective pins. The programming that is to be done is in low-level machine language so that the code can be interpreted by the hardware chip. Despite all the difficulties in implementing the entire model, the level of integration becomes easy with the usage of ESP8266 as it has an embedded chip used for electronics which are produced in mass. Having referenced that, it becomes hard for understudies, who need to explore different avenues regarding their thoughts with the assistance of IoT innovation. Hailed on the grounds that the driver of the Fourth Industrial Revolution, web of Things innovation has proactively found business use in regions practically identical to great stopping accuracy farming and water use the board. The serious examination has furthermore been directed into the work of IoT for creating canny frameworks in regions as well as hold-up minimization, underlying wellbeing checking, crash-keeping away from vehicles and savvy lattices.

9.3. System Architecture and Components

A system for monitoring a child's hydration level and oxygen saturating is designed and implemented. In this system, the Node MCU is used for collecting and processing all data received from the sensors attached [5] to the system which are DHT11 (for hydration and temperature) and MAX30100 (for oxygen density). The DHT11 sensor would be attached with a pacifier, and the pacifier would be attached with a playful ring which would be placed on the child's finger, where the ring would contain the oxygen sensor (MAX30100), which would collect the data from the child's body. All this data would be uploaded to the blynk application for immediate analysis. If the data achieved from the body by the sensors [6] exceed or succeed the critical limit, as implemented in the code for the application, an alert notification would be sent to the parent's phone by the help of which they would take further actions. An ESP8266 module is used for connecting the device to the internet connection. A battery of 3.7V would be connected with a 10K Ohm resistor. A voltage regulator (LM1117) would also be connected to the system along with a capacitor with 1000uF and 25V.

Wi-Fi Chip (ESP8266)

The plan of the prototyping source is accessible for Node MCU which is open-source and it is firmware. The Node MCU implies the firmware rather than the related advancement packs, its name comprises of two sections, one is the "Hub" and the other one is the "MCU" which represents a miniature regulator unit. This two expressed firmware and its prototyping board alongside its opened plan sources. The firmware as expressed before utilizes the prearranging language named Lua. The assembled firmware depends on the venture named eLua task, and this is based on the Espressif Non-OS programming improvement pack for the ESP8266 module. Many open-source activities, for example, lua-cjson and SPIEFS are being utilized by the ESP8266 module. Since there are asset limitations, the clients who expect to utilize the ESP8266 module need to choose the separate modules which are important for their undertakings and afterwards they need to construct a firmware for a similar which would additionally help in the fulfilment of the venture. 32-bit ESP32 support has likewise been carried out. The regular prototyping equipment which is being involved is a circuit board that capabilities as a double in-line package (DIP) which is utilized for the combination of a USB regulator which has a more modest surface and is mounted on a board containing the MCU alongside the radio wire. The DIP design that is chosen improves on the prototyping which is to be finished on the breadboards. The plan which was at first done depended on the ESP-12 module which has a place with the ESP8266, and which is a Wi-Fi SoC that is coordinated with a TensilicaXtensa LX106 centre, that is enormously utilized in the IoT application areas (See Figure 9.1 and 9.2).

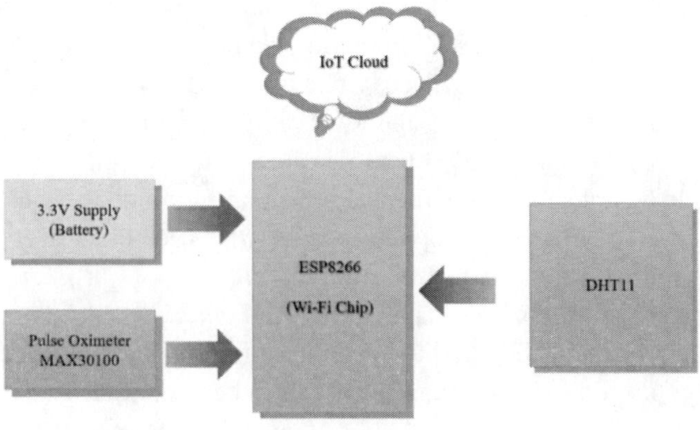

Figure 9.1. Proposed system.

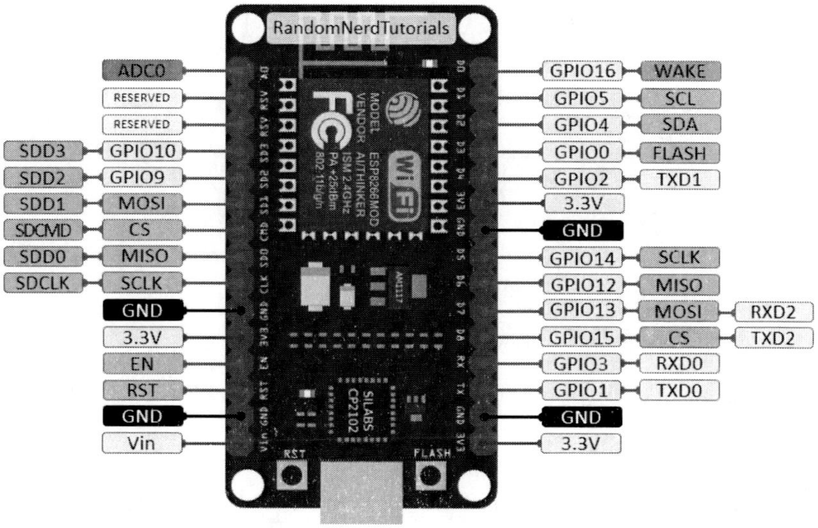

Figure 9.2. Components of Node MCU (ESP8266).

Pulse Oximeter Sensor

The oxygen that is taken by the body during respiration goes into the lungs and afterwards, it passes through the bloodstream. The blood vessels then carry the oxygen via arteries and veins to every organ present in our body for the process of metabolism. The best way through which oxygen is carried out in the blood is through the formation of oxyhemoglobin which is an unstable compound formed by the combination of oxygen and an iron compound in the blood known as haemoglobin. During the usage of a pulse oximeter, the reading is taken when a clamp-like structured device is placed on and above a finger, earlobe, or toe from where the oxygen saturation is evaluated. Small light beams are passed through the blood that is flowing through the finger where the device is placed, thereby measuring the amount of oxygen present in that bloodstream. This process is done by measuring the changes that happen in the light absorption in oxygenated or deoxygenated blood that is flowing through the vein or artery of the respective body part (for this device, the child's finger) (See Figure 9.3).

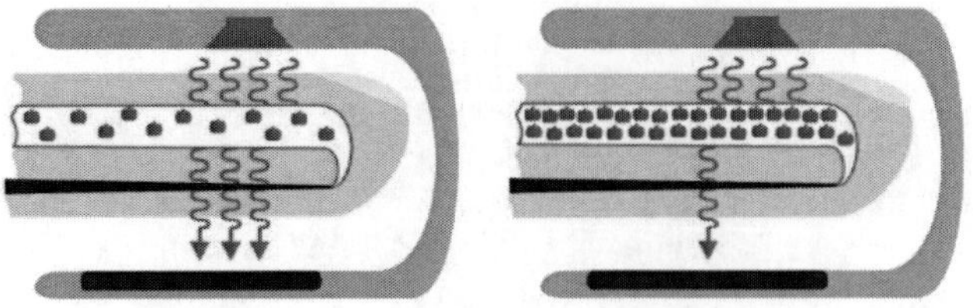

Figure 9.3. Comparison of two fingers inside the oximeter device: One with low oxygen saturation and another with high oxygen saturation.

The sensor that is used for calculating the pulse oximeter is MAX30100. This sensor is an integration of pulse oximetry and a heart-rate monitor sensor together which thereby calculated both the oxygen saturation and the pulse rate of the patient. It is a combination of two LEDs, where these are used as a photodetector, optimized optics, and a low-noise analog signal processor that detects the pulse rate and the heart-rate signals. Its operation range is from 1.8V and 3.3V power supplies and it can receive power down with the help of software which has a negligible standby current, and a permitting power supply that helps to connect at all times. Its shutdown current is ultra-low (0.7μA, type). It has a fast data output capability and its interface type is I2C. Since the device contains two LEDs, where one emits red light, and the other emits infrared light. For calculating the pulse rate, only infrared light is used. To measure the oxygen level in the bloodstream, both red light, as well as infrared light, is used. When the heart starts pumping blood, the level of oxygen increases, thereby increasing the quantity of oxygenated blood. As the heart relaxes after pumping, the volume of oxygenated blood is decreased. By calculating the time between the increase and decrease in the level of oxygenated blood, the pulse rate is calculated.

Figure 9.4. MAX30100 sensor.

It has been discovered that the ventilated blood absorbs a lot of actinic rays and then passes more red light whereas deoxygenated blood absorbs the red light and passes more infrared light. the most operate of MAX30100 is this, that is: it evaluates the absorption levels of each of the sunshine rays and then stores them in an exceedingly buffer space which will be red via the I2C protocol for communication (See Figure 9.4).

DHT11 Sensor

This is a sensor utilized for deciding the temperature and mugginess or dampness content. The DHT11 sensor module is a fundamental sensor module which consolidates a super minimal expense computerized temperature and a moistness sensor. It has the use of a capacitive moistness sensor and a thermistor which estimates the encompassing where it is kept and gives out a computerized signal on the information pin in the Node MCU module (simple information pins are not needed). It is exceptionally easy to utilize, however it requires cautious timing to get and assess the information accomplished. You can get another arrangement of information from the sensor at regular intervals, so when this sensor is utilized, a library is utilized from Adafruit, with the assistance of which the sensor readings can be saved is as long as 2 seconds old. This sensor accompanies a scope of 4.7K or 10K resistors, which will require a pullup from the information pin to VCC. This sensor has a scope of 3 to 5V power and info yield. A most extreme current of 2.5mA is consumed during a discussion that is while mentioning information. It has 4 pins joined to it with 0.1" separating (See Figure 9.5).

Figure 9.5. DHT11 sensor.

Battery

A 3.7V battery is being used. Lithium-ion (Li-ion) batteries have now become the most preferred source of power in most of the latest IoT applications and devices as they offer one of the best combinations of that power which is available per unit mass and volume. It is also a significant point to mention that is, this Li-ion battery has the highest coulometric efficiency. This means, that for every watt of power that is being put into a Li-ion battery one will get the maximum power back out. A single Li-ion cell nominally operates at 3.7V. This value is above the last popular cell marked at 3.3V which has been one of the most common in the logic levels used in the department of electronics in the present world today. Lead-acid batteries can provide more energy but at a lower temperature range than that Li-ion, which is the reason why they are still in use and are utilized in the automotive and also in grid storage industry. Though Nickel-cadmium batteries are well suited for low-temperature operation, however, similar to other nickel-based batteries, they are also very likely to have too high self-discharge. It is very highly advisable that no battery is to be charged at a low-temperature range, otherwise, this can damage these batteries permanently (See Figure 9.6).

Figure 9.6. Lithium ion battery.

Resistor

The resistor used here is the 10K ohm resistor. This Resistor is used to control the collector current which is passed through the transistor and it affects the bias point. Hence, according to the GAIN which is the specific amplification, which the designer wants, that has to be chosen for this resistor to be 10k by using the basic form of the transistor equations. A resistor is a component which has two passive terminals which include the electrical component that implements the resistance which is in the form of electrical resistance and is used as a circuit element. Resistors that are used in the electronic circuits, are used for reducing the current flow, it adjusts the level of signals, it helps to divide the voltages that are being used, it biases the active elements and also help in terminating the transmission lines, these are some of the main usages of the resistors among many others. There are high-power resistors, that help in the dissipation of higher or many watts of electrical power in the form of heat, which heat on the other hand can be used as a part of motor controls, in the systems which consist of the power distribution mechanism or can also be used as test loads for the generators. Stating about the fixed resistors, they have resistances that do not change noticeably, the only change that is seen is concerning the temperature, the time duration or the voltage that it's been operated in. On the other hand, stating the variable resistors helps in adjusting the circuit elements, such as a lamp dimmer or volume control. It can also be used as a sensing device, it can sense heat, humidity, light, chemical activity, force and many others. (Resistors are the common elements which form electronic networks, the electronic circuits, and are one of the main components of electronic equipment. Practical resistors are categorized as discrete components that can be composed of various forms and compounds. When an integrated circuit is developed, resistors are implemented in it because of its stated uses. The resistance specifies the electrical function of that of a resistor. The resistance range within the manufacturing tolerance is where the normal value of the resistance falls, it is indicated on the component (See Figure 9.7).

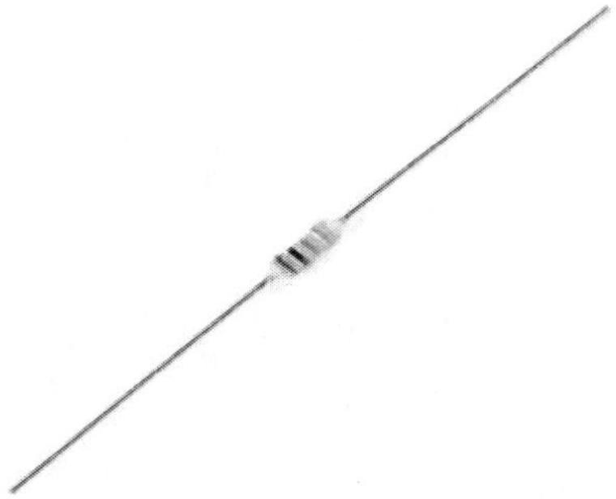

Figure 9.7. Resistor 10k ohm.

Voltage Regulator

A 3.3V controller is being utilized. The voltage controller chip named LM1117 is utilized in the proposed gadget. To keep a steady voltage, a voltage controller framework is planned. A voltage controller might be utilized for a straightforward feed-forward plan system or it might incorporate the component of negative input. The electromechanical instrument or the electronic parts can be utilized by the voltage controller. Contingent upon the proposed plan, the voltage controller may be utilized for managing single or numerous voltages which could either be an AC voltage or a DC voltage. The use of electronic voltage controllers is found in gadgets like the power supplies of the PCs, where they are utilized to balance out the DC voltages that are being utilized by the processor and different components which are utilized simultaneously. In focal power station generator plants and auto alternators, voltage controllers are accustomed to controlling the whole result of the plant. There may be an establishment of the voltage controllers in the substation of an electric power appropriation framework or along the dissemination lines with the goal that the clients get consistent voltage autonomy of how much power is to be drawn from the line. The LM1117, which is for the most part utilized in the IoT gadgets that have the necessity for a voltage controller is a low dropout voltage controller which has a dropout of 1.2 V at 800 mA of burden current. The LM1117 that is utilized is likewise accessible in a movable rendition, which assists with setting the resulting voltage from a reach of1.25 to 13.8 V with the utilization of just two outer resistors. What's more, these are accessible in five voltages that have a decent worth, for example, 1.8 V, 2.5 V, 3.3 V, and 5 V. Voltage controllers are significantly arranged into two fundamental classifications, one is the direct voltage controller and the other is the exchanging voltage controller. Both these sorts of voltage controllers direct a framework's voltage. Straight controllers work with low proficiency while exchanging controllers work with high productivity. With high-effectiveness exchanging voltage controllers, the greater part of the information power is brought to the result without misfortunes (see Figure 9.8).

Figure 9.8. Voltage regulator (LM1117).

Electrolytic Capacitor

The electrolyte capacitor that's used is 1000uF and a pair of 5V. 1000uF 25V capacitor is one of the high-quality electrolytic capacitors that are out there within the market that provides long life and also offers high reliability. These electrolytic capacitors are the foremost usually used sort of capacitors that are employed in Electronic Circuits. The electrolytic capacitors accommodate Polars, one is the Positive pole and another is the Negative pole. n associate electrolytic capacitor is additionally called a polarized capacitor that has an anode or a positive plate consisting of a metal that forms a chemical compound layer that acts as associate stuff via the method of anodization. This chemical compound layer then acts because of the dielectric portion of the electrical condenser. The physical states are equivalent to a solid, a liquid, or a gel sort of solution that covers the surface of the oxide layer present thereby serving itself as the cathode or the negative plate of this capacitor used. As there's a presence of a skinny dielectric oxide layer and its enlarged anode surface and also the electrolytic capacitors have a comparative higher capacitance-voltage (CV) product that is per unit volume as compared to the film capacitors or the ceramic capacitors, so it will then have large values of capacitance. The big capacitance that's gifted within the electrolytic capacitors, it makes them particularly appropriate for passing or bypassing frequencies that are of low signals, and it's used for storing large amounts of energy. Electrolytic capacitors are the polarized parts present since they need an asymmetrical construction that has to be operated with the presence of upper voltage which implies a lot of electric charge on the anode compared to it on the cathode throughout all times. These are high-quality 1000uF/25V electrolytic capacitors that are radial. These work very well as voltage noise suppressors used for voltage regulators and conjointly for power offers. Golf shot one in all these mentioned on top of across power and another within the ground in every one of the projects, ensuring a sleek noise-resistant power supply that also has larger reliability (See Figure 9.9).

Figure 9.9. Electrolytic capacitor (1000uf and 25V).

9.4. Working Principle

The device is so constructed that it gets placed on the finger of the child and the sensors attached to the device capture the information from the body and shows it in the associated mobile application. The entire system has the following components: The Wi-Fi chip which is the ESP8266 module, the pulse oximeter sensor which is the MAX30100 chip, the temperature-humidity sensor which is the DHT11 chip, a battery of 3.7V, a resistor of 10K ohm, a voltage regulator which is the LM1117 and the electrolytic capacitor of 1000uF, 25V. Module ESP8266 is connected with the DHT11 sensor and the MAX30100 for the calculation of the oxygen saturation, humidity and temperature of the child. The values of temperature and humidity are received from the child's mouth where the DHT11 sensor is attached near the tip of the pacifier and the value of the oxygen saturation of the child's body is estimated with the help of the MAX30100 sensor which would be attached to the top part of the pacifier which would have a ring-like structure that would be placed or attached to the child's finger. The data received by the Wi-Fi module via the sensors are transferred to the Blynk application. Now if the values fall or rise above the critical temperature, humidity or oxygen saturation level, then notification would be sent to the parent's mobile where the respective Blynk application is being downloaded. The values are evaluated and judged by a professional, such as a doctor for further procedures and treatments (See Figure 9.10).

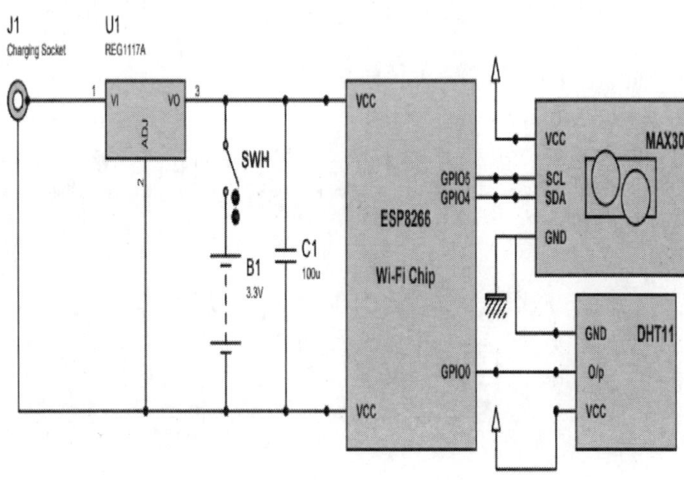

Figure 9.10. Circuit diagram.

9.5. Implementation

The DHT11 sensor is attached to the surface of the pacifier which touches the face of the child to achieve the correct hydration level and temperature of the child from the touch of the pacifier to the child's mouth. The MAX30100 is attached to the other face of the pacifier and the bottom side of the finger ring is attached to the pacifier to get the oxygen level in the blood by passing a small beam of light (which is the mechanism of the pulse oximeter). With the help of these sensors, the values of hydration level, temperature and oxygen saturation are calculated. These sensors are linked to a control unit, which computes the values of all the sensors. These calculated values are then conveyed to the Blynk application. From the application, the values are then accessed by the doctor and patient. Thus, based on the temperature, hydration level and oxygen saturation values, the doctor can decide the state of the child and appropriate measures can be taken (See Figure 9.11 and 9.12).

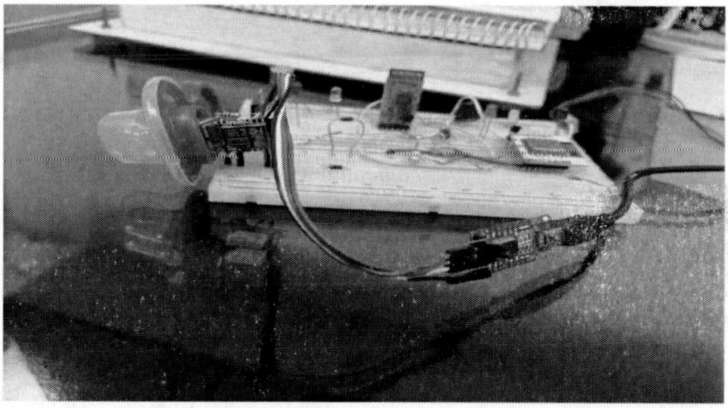

Figure 9.11. Device being coded with FTDI.

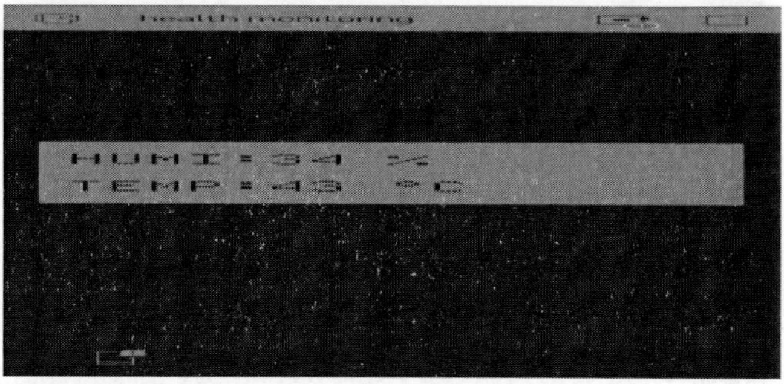

Figure 9.12. Display of data in the Blynk application.

9.6. Application Area

Continuous care and monitoring of children can prevent serious conditions such as dehydration and problems related to asphyxia which leads to the death of children approximately 5 million every year, globally. So, the technology based on the Internet of Things related to child health monitoring systems would be the most appropriate solution for it. This device would help the care providers to evaluate and monitor a child with many conditions in a remote manner with the help of virtual channels such as—phone, email, video consultations, portable medical devices, home health kits, etc.—when the child remains safely at the comfort of their home. These systems enable alerts notification to the parents of the concerned child if the data evaluated are out of the normal range of values. Remote patient (children in this case) monitoring allows parents or the doctors they consult to

- Readjust the dosing of the medication given or the methods of the treatment that is regularly given to improve the health condition
- Minimize the requirement of hospitalizations by timely checking the received data as soon as the alert notification indicates a problem
- The progress of the patient can be monitored to improve the treatment process
- Priority can be given to the urgent concern of the patient due to the availability of required data
- Provide a proper and intensive overview of the patient's health
- Reduces the requirement of manual data collection and data entry, which further provides more data for analysis to improvise the decisions of a doctor. The main goal of RPM (Remote Patient Monitoring) is to ensure that all patients and children who are prone to severe illness, can have remote regular checkup systems with the help of which the regular trend of change in data evaluated can be stored for future reference and future decision making of the professionals.

Conclusion

The Internet of Things (IoT) is one rising technology that has attracted great attention in current past years for its tremendous potential to improve the problems of the healthcare sector which is caused by an ageing population and which thereby has greatly risen the numbers of chronic illness in the population. Similarly, this IoT-based device can prevent the death of children below the age of 5 years. Children below the age of 5 years are not able to convey their requirements to their parents, such as if they are thirsty or if they are having a minor breading problem. They might cry but due to a lack of communication translation, parents or the child's caretaker would feed them to make them stop crying instead of understanding the greater cause behind it. This leads to the problem remaining unsolved. Continuation of this problem leads to fatal issues that might also lead to the death of the infant. These problems are the cause of the death of approximately 5 million children every year, globally. Since the sensors are implemented on a pacifier, which is of a child's interest, he/she will always play with it, thereby leading to the collection of the required data from the child. This device would be an improved version of the already existing device which is popular globally. If the data increases or decreases below the critical level as stated in the programming as per the medical norms, it notifies the concerned parent or guardian who then takes care of the child as per the requirement, or if required, the child is taken to the doctor.

References

[1] Perrier, E. (2015). *Positive Disruption: Healthcare Ageing and Participation in the Age of Technology*, Sydney, NSW, Australia: The McKell Institute.

[2] Gope, P. and Hwang, T. (Mar, 2016). "BSN-care: A secure IoT-based modern healthcare system using body sensor network", *IEEE Sensors J.*, vol. 16, pp. 1368-1376.

[3] Pasluosta, C. F., Gassner, H., Winkler, J., Klucken, J., and Eskofier, B. M. (Nov, 2015). "An emerging era in the management of Parkinson's disease: Wearable technologies and the Internet of Things", *IEEE J. Biomed. Health Inform.*, vol. 19, no. 6, pp. 1873-1881.

[4] Fan, Y. J., Yin, Y. H., Xu, L. D., Zeng, Y., and Wu, F. (May, 2014). "IoT-based smart rehabilitation system", *IEEE Trans. Ind. Informat.*, vol. 10, no. 2, pp. 1568-1577.

[5] Sarkar, S., and Misra, S. (Jan./Feb., 2016). "From micro to nano: The evolution of wireless sensor-based health care", *IEEE Pulse*, vol. 7, no. 1, pp. 21-25.

[6] Poon, C. C. Y., Lo, B. P. L., Yuce, M. R., Alomainy, A., and Hao, Y. (2015). "Body sensor networks: In the era of big data and beyond", *IEEE Rev. Biomed. Eng.*, vol. 8, pp. 4-16.

Chapter 10

Internet of Robotics Things (IoRT) in Healthcare Systems

Deepak Rao Khadatkar*
and Yogesh Kumar Rathore†
Department of Computer Science and Engineering,
Shri Shankaracharya Institute of Professional Management and Technology,
Raipur (C.G.), India

Abstract

The Internet of Things (IoT) and Artificial Intelligence (AI) are the fastest-growing technologies in the medical field. There are so many devices available in the market to serve patients, especially from remote areas. Some existing devices like Oximeters, Blood pressure watches, fitness trackers, EEG hand bands, and IoT robots are used to capture real-time information about a patient, then these data need to be processed to detect health-related issues of a person at an early stage. In this chapter, we want to put focus on such devices with their challenges and limitations, and also focus on how the artificial intelligence-based model can process such data and help physicians and doctors to detect any possible disease. Through this chapter, we also tried to introduce the unrevealed field of IoRT (Internet of Robotics Things) in healthcare. The gaps identified in this chapter may be helpful for further research to design and update the IoT devices used in the healthcare sector.

Keywords: internet of things, robots, healthcare, clinical data handling

---

* Corresponding Author's Email: d.khadatkar@ssipmt.com.
† Corresponding Author's Email: y.rathore@ssipmt.com.

In: Applications of Artificial Intelligence in the Healthcare Sector
Editors: Jyoti Prakash Patra and Yogesh Kumar Rathore
ISBN: 979-8-88697-502-4

10.1. Introduction

Internet of Things (IoT) in healthcare has enormous implicit to transfigure medical treatment and boost global health. In this chapter we've covered multitudinous seeing technologies in health- acquainted mobile operations, and wearable bias similar to fitness trackers, pulse oximeters, blood pressure watches, EEG headbands and numerous robotic devices used in healthcare. Some of them are used in hospitals to cover medical pointers, and we use others freely to track real-time health data when we're at home or in the office. The junction of data engineering with IoT can ameliorate the remote monitoring of any case, therefore, serving the healthcare area in the best suitable way. IoT devices can be applied to cover numerous pointers and can use the live data to get the accompanied terrain between cases and croaker [1]. In this way, we can collect and maintain a huge quantum of medical data with maximum delicacy. While the healthcare sector is being converted by the capability to record massive quantities of information about individual cases, the huge volume of data being collected is insolvable for mortal beings to dissect. Machine literacy provides us with numerous methodologies and ways for assaying different conditions, which enables healthcare professionals to diagnose a case veritably precisely and directly. There are numerous possibilities for how machine literacy can be used in healthcare, and all of them depend on having sufficient data and authorization to use it [2].

Robotics is an area of computer science that studies how to make machines behave in a way that would appear intelligent to the observer. The term robotics gets come under the AI banner, but not all robots are smart, a robot is a machine that does work by itself following a set of rules programmed by a computer. Robots are common in manufacturing but they are also developing in other fields like education and health where they operate directly alongside a human in the classrooms or in operation rooms [3].

Figure 10.1, cycle shows the working cycle of an IoT device, where sensors are used to collect the patient data like, pulse rate, body temperature, blood pressure etc. then these data send to the monitoring system using the internet, cloud or Bluetooth. Finally, the monitor collects the data and processes the data to make the decision, if it is an expert system it can suggest the treatment by itself, and if it is not an expert system it may send the data to a doctor for further processing. Nowadays, robots are used as monitoring systems which are not only capable of taking decisions but can also perform the task of a doctor by themselves [4].

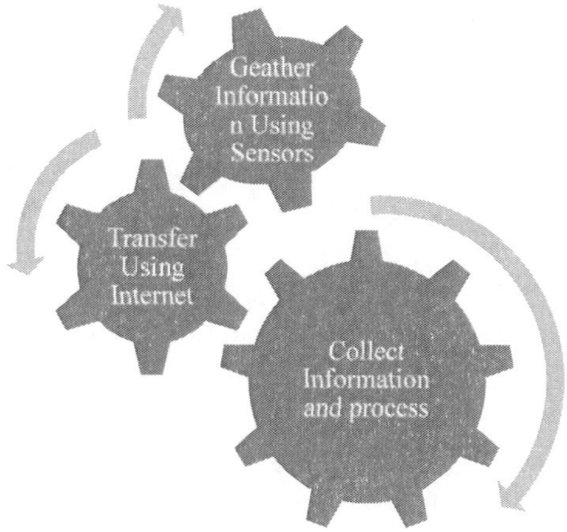

Figure 10.1. Working of IoT devices in healthcare.

10.1.1. Gather Information Using Sensors

The Internet of Things (IoT) is typically defined as uniquely identifiable endpoints and/or objects that are linked through one or more networks. The technology has a wide range of applications and is used for a variety of purposes, in different fields. Medical devices that collect data on patients are called sensors. These include pulse oximeters, electrocardiograms, thermometers, fluid level sensors, sphygmomanometers (blood pressure monitors) and so forth.

10.1.2. Transfer Data Using the Internet (Connectivity)

IoT system provides better connectivity of devices or sensors from the microcontroller to the server and also from server to microcontroller to read and write data respectively. For all these connectivity it uses Bluetooth, WiFi, etc.

10.1.3. Collect Information and Process

The healthcare system analyzes data from sensors to see how the patient is functioning. If there is a problem, the system can tell a doctor what part of the body is affected, so the doctor can provide advice on how to remedy the problem [5].

10.2. Literature Survey

IoT systems are used in various ways to help doctors to collect information about the patient. IoT-based robots are programmed and trained using artificial intelligence and are capable of taking data from the cloud and processing the data. Currently, it has been used in several medical applications such as measurement of the sugar level, body temperature, pulse rate, oxygen level etc. along with monitoring of patient activity, abnormal activities on hospital premises and cleaning and security of the clinic [6, 7]. It is always good to use mobile robots in place of sensors because sensors are bulky and need too much power and connectivity to transfer data. Furthermore, the data gathered by the sensor send to the local host to store from where a robot can pick the data to process. In this way, we can save the time needed [8]. Hence, while designing IoT-based robots once need to keep in mind to maintain distributed information to ensure data availability and delivery [9]. The critical thinking and decision capability make a robot realize its connection with the atmosphere or with a particular object. There are different aspects of cognition including observation, intelligence, processing of information, analysis, problem-solving, and opinion [10]. In an IoT-aided robotic atmosphere, the robot uses clouds, storage and surroundings to gain knowledge e.g., the human body, cameras, and sensors installed in different locations [11].

10.3. IoRT (Internet of Robotics Things) Devices in the Healthcare

10.3.1. Implantable Glucose Monitoring Systems

Many persons are suffering from diabetes nowadays; they can have a small device just under their skin which contains a miniature form of the sensor attached to it. This small device can continuously monitor the sugar level of the body and then this sensor in the device will send data to the mobile phone of the user and can also have a history of daily data in the cloud. Using a device like this a patient can manage or can better control his regular glucose level for a better life.

10.3.2. Activity Trackers during Cancer Treatment

Cancer patients can also have regular monitoring of their weight and age because a better treatment of the cancer patient mostly relies on his or her weight and age. The daily routine and lifecycle of the person also play an important role in the treatment of cancer like if we have a record of daily movement, fatigue level, eating habits etc. then a better treatment plan can be created for the patient. So the activity tracker is a device which can track patients all the above-stated things. Plus, the data which are collected can also be sent to the professionals so that they suggest proper medicine for better treatment. Doctors can also use this prior and after treatment record of the patient recorded by the activity tracker to deal with further follow-ups.

10.3.3. IoT-Based Heart Disease Monitoring System

Heart diseases are more common these days, so many companies discovered heart disease monitoring system which is capable of calculating the function of the heart by using data like pulse rate, sugar level, ECG, EEG Signals, Blood pressure etc. and provides suggestion or generate an alert system for doctors or family members [12].

10.3.4. Medical Alert Systems

Some medical tracking devices look like a piece of jewellery only so no one can even notice that you have to wear medical tracking equipment but actually, these devices are designed to alert family members or friends nearby in case of an emergency. For instance, if a person who is wearing a medical alert bracelet, watch or a pendent-like thing and fell out of bed in the middle of the night, or got some accident then an emergency notification will be sent to the people's smartphones the person is already in prior designated to help in the case of an emergency.

10.3.5. Ingestible Sensors

In our body, some parts are where devices can not reach to take data. IoT suggests some ingestible sensors which can go to the most unreachable parts of the body and can provide us with data which are required for better treatment. This archetype will allow for direct access to the body parts during the passage of ingestible. Because these sensors come in the form of little capsules only, they can be easily swallowed by a person. Once the sensors are ingested, they start sending information to a patient's mobile app, by using the data a patient can easily monitor the internal conditions of the body and can follow the proper dosages for their medications. Some ingestible sensors are also being used to more accurately diagnose patients with things like irritable bowel syndrome and colon cancer. These types of sensors are not really harmful because they don't stay in the body for much time, they just went out with the body waste material.

10.3.6. Traceable Inhalers

Sometimes breathing conditions are to be monitored for better handling of asthma patients. IoT inhalers are the devices which tell asthma patients what they're doing or experiencing prior to causing asthma attacks, by providing information to their smartphones. This data can also be shared with the related doctors so that regular examinations can also be done. These inhalers are also able to remind the patients to take their medicines at the proper time.

10.3.7. Wearables to Fight Depressions

Depression patients can also have IoT devices for proper monitoring. In today's era due to work pressure, and a fast lifestyle many people face the problem of depression. Sometimes people may fall down or blackout due to depression and commit suicide also in some cases. So, it becomes very necessary to monitor the mental health of such patients regularly, to deal with such problems one of the leading mobile and telecommunication companies Apple has specially designed an app for its Apple Watch that helps manic-depressive patients cope with their depression. The app can monitor the person's mood in a different situation, and how he/she reacts in a different condition. The app tracks a patient's mood outside of their scheduled appointments and helps to monitor cognitive functions.

10.3.8. Robots in Healthcare

During Pandemic COVID-19, the demand for robots in the field of healthcare rapidly increased because robots can easily stop the chain of human transferable diseases. Thereafter, lots of experiments were done in the field of artificial intelligence to include robots for many different purposes. Some robots are used as an assistant, some robots are used to handle clinical data and some expert robots are also used to help doctors in surgery. In a short period, the use of robots rapidly increase in healthcare but there are some challenges in handling accuracy, time and decision-making capabilities in robots [12].

- Decision-making capabilities

  In healthcare, decision-making is a crucial task because one needs to make decisions quickly and precisely to serve better to their patients. To make robots capable of decision-making similar to a doctor, lots of expert systems have been used to train the robots to make a robot capable of taking critical decisions. The working cycle of IoRT (Internet of Robotics Things) is shown in Figure 10.2.
- Accuracy

  Accuracy is another big issue need to handle while using robots in healthcare because false prediction and action may lead to harm to human life. So, to increase accuracy in work a robot is trained with a large amount of data from the relevant field. To train a robot massive amount of data is needed. That's why most robots make for special purposes only some are used to serve medicines, some are used to suggest medicine, some are used for surgery, and some are used to handle medical data. According to need, the robots are trained with lots of data from the relevant field.
- Flexibility

  If we are using a robot for any surgery then it must be flexible enough to pick the knife, scissors and other medical equipment. This needs lots of small components to connect together like the human body, also needs to program a lot to work as a human being.

- Perception and Interaction

  Robots should be able to learn from the environment and perceive information from the environment so that, they will be capable enough to take decisions. It takes information in the form of numerical data, text data and images from multiple sensors then it manipulates the information and took the decision based on training [13].

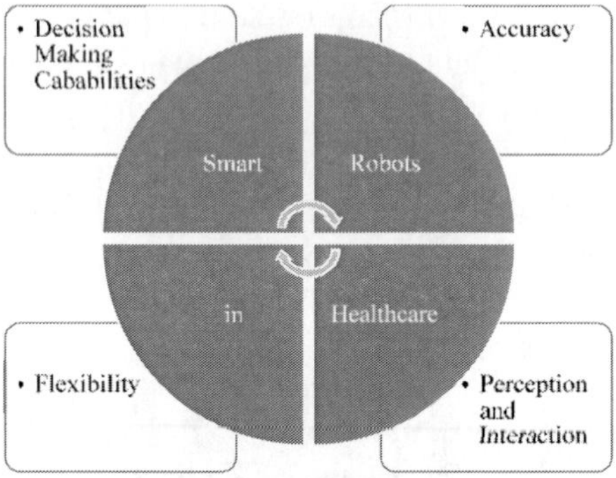

Figure 10.2. Working of robots in the healthcare.

10.4. Challenges

The application of IoT and Robots is rapidly increasing in the healthcare sector and converting the healthcare sector towards automation. At the same time, its use needs to deal with many challenges like decision-making capabilities, providing robust network to transfer information, data handling and analysis, and cost-effectiveness. Nowadays needs and requirements rapidly changing in the field of healthcare, So IoT devices need to upgrade their selves as per the requirement of the environment, similarly, robots need to make different decisions as per the condition of the patients having the same disease. The cost of the robot and training of the robot is again a big challenge in this domain.

Conclusion

The success of any IoT device or IoRT device is always measured on the basis of accuracy, cost-effectiveness and flexibility to make changes in the device.

The current devices are capable of doing things nicely but some issues like dependencies on power and the internet make them a thread in the healthcare industry. The accuracy of data and processing time of data also became very important in the field of healthcare as these data may save someone life. The current robotic system has some limitations in terms of customization because healthcare domain needs lots of customization frequently due to rapid change in equipment and technology. Also, treatment may vary from person to person so decision-making capability also needs to enhance. So today's robots must have flexible enough to get adjusted as per the need of the doctor and patient.

References

[1] Botterman, Maarten. "*Internet of Things: an early reality of the Future Internet, European Commission*." Information Society and Media Directorate General, Networked Enterprise & RFID Unit (D4) (2009).

[2] Patel, Ankit R., Rajesh S. Patel, Navdeep M. Singh, and Faruk S. Kazi. "Vitality of robotics in healthcare industry: an Internet of Things (IoT) perspective." In *Internet of Things and Big Data Technologies for Next Generation Healthcare,* pp. 91-109. Springer, Cham, 2017.

[3] Butter, M., Rensma, A., van Boxsel, J., Kalisingh, S., Schoone, M., et al.: *Robotics for healthcare—final report,* p. 12. European Commission, DG Information Society, Brussels (2008).

[4] Wang, Mingzhong, Chongdan Pan, and Pradeep Kumar Ray. "Technology entrepreneurship in developing countries: Role of telepresence robots in healthcare." *IEEE Engineering Management Review* 49, no. 1 (2021): 20-26.

[5] Pang, Zhibo, Qiang Chen, Junzhe Tian, Lirong Zheng, and Elena Dubrova. "Ecosystem analysis in the design of open platform-based in-home healthcare terminals towards the internet-of-things." In *2013 15th international conference on advanced communications technology (ICACT),* pp. 529-534. IEEE, 2013.

[6] Taylor, R. H., A. Menciassi, G. Fichtinger, P. Fiorini, and P. Dario, "Medical robotics and computer-integrated surgery," *Springer Handbook of Robotics,* Springer, Cham, Switzerland, 2016.

[7] Fleming, M., A. Patrick, M. Gryskevicz et al., "Deployment of a touchless ultraviolet light 13robot for terminal room disinfection: the importance of audit and feedback," *American Journal of Infection Control,* vol. 46, no. 2, pp. 241–243, 2018.

[8] Remy, S. L. and M. B. Blake, "Distributed service-oriented robotics," *IEEE Internet Computing*, vol. 15, no. 2, pp. 70–74, 2011.

[9] Thrun, S. "Simultaneous localization and mapping," in *Robotics and Cognitive Approaches to Spatial Mapping,* pp. 13–41, Springer, Berlin, Germany, 2007.

[10] Vanderelst, D. and A. Winfield, "An architecture for ethical robots inspired by the simulation theory of cognition," *Cognitive Systems Research,* vol. 48, pp. 56–66, 2018.

[11] Burghart, C., R. Mikut, R. Stiefelhagen et al., "A cognitive architecture for a humanoid robot: a first approach," in *Proceedings of the 5th IEEE-RAS International Conference on Humanoid Robots*, pp. 357–362, IEEE, Tsukuba, Japan, December 2005.

[12] Premebida, C., R. Ambrus, and Z.-C. Marton, "Intelligent robotic perception systems," in *Applications of Mobile RobotsIntechOpen,* London, UK, 2018.

[13] Hadidi, R., J. Cao, M. Woodward, M. S. Ryoo, H. Kim, and A. Letters, "Distributed perception by collaborative robots," *IEEE Robotics and Automation Letters*, vol. 3, no. 4, pp. 3709–3716, 2018.

Index

About the Editors

Dr. J. P. Patra is a Professor at Shri Shankaracharya Institute of Professional Management and Technology, Raipur under Chhattisgarh Swami Vivekanand Technical University, Bhilai, India. He holds more than 17 years of experience in research, teaching in these areas Artificial Intelligence, Analysis and Design of Algorithms, Cryptography and Network Security. He got acclaimed for being the author of the books Cognitive IoT: Emerging Technology towards Human Wellbeing (ISBN: 9781032315560), Analysis and Design of Algorithms (ISBN: 978-93-80674-53-7) and Performance Improvement of a Dynamic System Using Soft Computing Approaches (ISBN: 978-3-659-82968-0) along with has more than 51 papers published in SCI, SCOPUS, Web of Science and UGCCARE Listed Journals. He has Published and granted Indian/Australian patents. He has contributed to book chapters, published by Elsevier, Springer and IGI Global. He is associated with AICTE-IDEA LAB, IIT Bombay and IIT Kharagpur as a Coordinator. He is on the editorial board and Reviewer Board of four leading international journals. In addition, he is on the Technical Committee Board for several International Conferences. He is having a Life Membership in Professional bodies like CSI, ISTE, and QCFI, also he has served the post of Chairman of the Raipur Chapter for the Computer Society of India which is India's Largest Professional body for Computer Professionals. He has served in various positions in different Engineering colleges as Associate Professor and Head. Currently, he is working with SSIPMT, Raipur as a Professor & Head in the Department of Computer Science & Engineering.

Yogesh Kumar Rathore received M. Tech. degree in Computer Science Engineering from Chhattisgarh Swami Vivekanand Technical University, Bhilai, India in the year 2010.He has 16 years experience of working, as an Assistant Professor (Department of Computer Science Engineering) at Shri Shankaracharya Institute of Professional Management and Technology, Raipur. Currently, he is also a Ph.D. scholar (part-time) at the Department of Information Technology, National Institute of Technology, Raipur. He has published more than 40 research papers in various conferences and journals including Scopus and SCI index. He has also published many book chapters in the books of international publishers like Springer, IGI global etc. and also published 2 patents on the topics "RIFT based automatic parking system for vehicle" and "AI-based Technique for Plant Disease identification". He has good hands-on C, MATLAB, IoT and Python programming language, which is the soul of many research in today's era. His interests include pattern recognition, image processing, Video Processing, Deep Learning, machine learning, and Artificial Intelligence.